vegan
bowls

Also by Zsu Dever

Everyday Vegan Eats

vegan
bowls

perfect flavor harmony
in cozy one-bowl meals

zsu dever

VEGAN HERITAGE PRESS

Woodstock • Virginia

ISBN 13: 978-1-941252-15-4
Second Printing, October 2015
10 9 8 7 6 5 4 3 2

Vegan Heritage Press, LLC books are available at quantity discounts. For information, please visit our website at www.veganheritagepress.com or write the publisher at Vegan Heritage Press, P.O. Box 628, Woodstock, VA 22664-0628.

Library of Congress Cataloging-in-Publication Data

Dever, Zsu, 1972-
  Vegan bowls : perfect flavor harmony in cozy one-bowl meals / Zsu Dever. -- First edition.
     pages cm
  Includes bibliographical references and index.
  ISBN 978-1-941252-15-4 (pbk. : alk. paper) -- ISBN 978-1-941252-16-1 (epub : alk. paper) -- ISBN 978-1-941252-17-8 (prc : alk. paper) 1. Vegan cooking. 2. One-dish meals. I. Title.
  TX837.D38 2015
  641.5'636--dc23
                        2015017269

Photo credits: Cover and interior food photography by Zsu Dever. Incidental spot photos from stock photo sources. **Cover Photo:** (front) Miso-Cajun Grilled Sweet Potato Bowl, page 101.

Disclaimer: The information provided in this book should not be taken as medical advice. If you require a medical diagnosis or prescription, or if you are contemplating any major dietary change, juice fast, or change in your exercise habits, consult a qualified health-care provider. You should always seek an expert medical opinion before making changes in your diet or supplementation regimen. Neither the publisher nor the author are responsible for readers' health issues.

Publisher's Note: The information in this book is correct and complete to the best of our knowledge. Website addresses and contact information were correct at the time of publication. The publisher is not responsible for specific health or allergy issues or adverse reactions to recipes contained in this book.

Vegan Heritage Press books are distributed by Andrews McMeel Publishing.

Printed in the United States of America

dedication

To my remarkable and brilliant children, Catt, Mikel, and Kati. Your support and encouragement have been invaluable and deeply appreciated. May your dreams, too, come true.

pasta e fagiole bowl (page 147)

contents

what's for dinner?

If the answer to this question is hard to come by, perhaps it's because life has again taken hold of your day and you're busy with everything from kids, family, work or school to social media, a good book, friends, cleaning, or maybe just the adorable cats on Instagram. We may only notice that it's dinnertime when the clock strikes a certain hour or our internal alarm goes off and the stomach starts to rumble. At that point, any lofty plans to spend a few hours in the kitchen cooking up a storm fly out the window.

So, what *is* for dinner? It can be restaurant food, convenience food in a box, or a can of beans and rice with a green salad (again). Of course, there is also the old stand-by peanut butter sandwich or bowl of cereal that I remember all too well from my college years.

What if I told you that tonight's dinner can be Veggie Lasagna or Sambal-Glazed Tempeh? How about Enchiladas with Pumpkin Cream Sauce or warming Tex-Mex Risotto? Now, what if I told you that all four of these dishes are complete meals served in a cozy bowl, with protein, starch, vegetables, and satisfying flavors and can be made in less time than it takes to pick up take-out?

It's true for all the recipes that I've hand-picked for this book of bowl meals. But these recipes are more than just meal components served in a bowl. I aim to show you that bowl food is way more than the sum of its parts. The recipes in this book are all about great food combinations and ingredients working in harmony. Where the ingredients might be ordinary when served separately, but when combined my way, the individual components of every *Vegan Bowls* meal complement each other in an exciting way.

Like all families, mine is swamped with sports, school, work, play, and much-needed family time. We don't have the luxury, especially during the week, of spending hours in the kitchen, so dinner has to be fast and convenient, but still wholesome and healthy.

Healthy meals are especially important in our busy, fast-paced lifestyles, and that's where this book can help. The recipes range from grilled dishes, grains, and sautés to breakfast bowls, dinner salads, hearty soups, and pastas. I share with you tips and tricks to help you get in and out of the kitchen fast. This gives you more time to enjoy your meal and your family, all the while cooking up healthy, great-tasting dishes.

With *Vegan Bowls* you can make satisfying, well-balanced meals that your family will love, using fresh, whole ingredients that require only a minimum amount of preparation time.

Welcome to my way of cooking and to my delicious bowl meals.

one | all about bowl food

The popularity of bowl meals is evidenced by the growing number of "bowls" featured on restaurant and food truck menus. When we tuck into a bowl meal, we have a few reasonable expectations. First, it should be uniquely satisfying. Second, it should be a complete meal, requiring nothing supplemental beyond, perhaps, an optional piece of crusty bread. In addition, the food should reflect a balance of flavors and textures. It should be easy to eat, seldom requiring more than a fork or spoon. And the bowl should be portable, allowing us to enjoy our meal anywhere, making for a casual mealtime experience.

With *Vegan Bowls* you can enjoy everything you love about bowl meals right in your own kitchen. In addition to satisfying these basic expectations, the bowl recipes in this book range from familiar comfort foods to creative, beyond-the-ordinary bowl meals.

On top of being delicious restaurant-quality meals, these cozy bowls can be ready in around 30 minutes. Special care was taken in composing these dishes, and the directions are precisely crafted to seamlessly flow from one component to the next. I have also included Quick Tips to help you get dinner, lunch, or breakfast on the table as quickly as possible, as well as suggestions tailored for each recipe. Because of the unique way in which the recipes are written, it is possible to go from cutting board to dinner table in record time.

This book is all about flavor, nutrition, speed, and balance. It's also unique in the sense that each of the more than ninety recipes is a complete meal in itself. The bowl components require no additional recipes with the exception of optional basics in chapter 2 that you might choose to make in advance.

Balance is the key to creating delicious and nutritious bowls. The tried-and-true bowl of rice, vegetables, and beans is the bowl-food blueprint, and it works beautifully. It contains protein, starch, and vegetables. Add a sauce to the bowl, and the separate components are now a harmonious unit. However, the recipes in this book are not just variations on replacing the beans with another protein or substituting another starch for the rice; these bowls go way beyond the scope of plain rice, beans, and vegetables.

This book presents three basic kinds of recipes:

- traditional
- semi-traditional
- original

The "traditional" bowls include such recipes as congee, which is made in almost every country in Asia, each region putting its own spin on this mainstay dish. Centuries of recipe development can't really be beat, but I've given these traditional recipes a few vegan tweaks to make them just right. Each one already contains a protein (albeit, in most cases, not vegan), a starch (typically rice), and some sort of vegetable.

The "semi-traditional" recipes are based on popular recipes that are almost "bowl" recipes already, so they need only a little adjustment. For example, Korean bulgogi is almost a complete meal in itself; I simply add a few elements while respecting the integrity the original dish.

The "original" recipes are those that I created in their entirety. As in all the other recipes, I've tried to create a balance among protein, starch, and vegetables while providing a range of satisfying flavors.

the components of a bowl recipe

When creating these bowl recipes, I kept in mind five essential components for making an ideal bowl meal:

- texture
- aroma
- color
- flavor combinations
- taste

Texture. Texture concerns mouthfeel and includes elements such as creaminess, crunchiness, chewiness and crispiness. A variety of textures in a single bowl enhances the experience of eating it. A bowl of puréed spinach topped with quinoa and a tahini sauce might be nutritionally sound, but has only one texture. Adding chopped almonds would vary the texture and therefore the eating experience. Kidney beans would add chewiness to the bowl and transform it into something pleasing to the palate.

Aroma. Aroma profiles are easy to work with because each ingredient conveys its own characteristics. The classic lemon, garlic, and oregano, for example, enliven your senses in a natural aroma harmony. The combinations in this book add to the overall enjoyment of each bowl meal.

Color. It is well known that the more colorful produce you eat, the better chance you have of obtaining an abundance of nutrients. I make sure to include a great variety of produce in these recipes, even ingredients you might not think go well together. It is all about the complete bowl. For instance, certain recipes call for the addition of earthy Swiss chard, while others need the balance of bitter collard greens. It is by careful design that each type of produce is chosen for each bowl. While some substitution is welcome, to maintain the best flavor of each bowl, I recommend using the called-for ingredients. Color, of course, is not just limited to produce. Legumes, sauces, and grains all have their own distinct hues, and each one brings its own dimension of flavor.

Flavor Combinations. Flavor combinations are probably the trickiest element of a dish to master. Not only do we all find various foods delicious, some ingredients just pair better with others. We see this time and again in classic combinations such as basil and tomato, lemon and garlic, black beans and sweet potatoes, smoke and collard greens, coconut milk and chile peppers, and summer squash, beans, and corn. Some ingredients simply combine well together, while others not so much. For me, combining flavors is the most fun aspect of creating recipes, but it is also the most challenging. I designed these recipes with flavor compatibility in mind.

Taste. Our tongues recognize the following taste sensations: sweetness, saltiness, sourness, bitterness, umami, piquancy, and temperature. How well these taste components are balanced goes a long way towards determining how well overall a dish works.

Sweetness can be supplied by granulated sugar or maple syrup, but it can also be supplied by caramelized onions or sweet potatoes. Even something as subtle as a pinch of sugar can round out the flavors of a dish, enhancing the other ingredients. I use caramelized onions in many recipes for a bit of sweetness without adding any actual sugary ingredient.

Saltiness can be supplied by salt, vegan cheeses, miso, pickles or tamari.

Sourness is just as important as saltiness. It is is achieved with ingredients such as the acidic fresh lemon juice and vinegars. Sourness can brighten other flavors, but it is an essential component when the dish itself is rich. Note that rich dishes are not necessarily fatty; chickpeas, potatoes, and paprika are "rich"-tasting ingredients that benefit from the addition of more tartness than most other dishes need. An example of this is the Chickpea Brasoi Bowl (page 59), which is a combination of chickpeas and sautéed potatoes in a thick garlic-paprika sauce. The flavors in this dish are delicious, but without any acid, the richness would be overwhelming. For that reason, I accompany the dish with an acidic salad that lightens the otherwise heavy legumes and potatoes.

Bitterness is the companion flavor to sweetness, as one can be balanced by the other. Bitterness is prevalent in dandelion greens, collard greens, and walnuts. In addition to sourness, bitterness also cuts through the richness of dishes.

Umami is the new kid on the block, at least in the West, but one that the culinary world has welcomed. It means "savoriness" or meatiness. It is a deep flavor that is brought about by ingredients such as fermented foods, miso, mushrooms, sea vegetables, and tomatoes.

Piquancy is spiciness, another important aspect of a well-balanced dish. A pinch of cayenne or red pepper flakes or a few slices of fresh chiles is all it takes to include it. While using just a little bit is essential, the complete absence of it is an obvious omission, even if you can't actually taste the spice. For this reason, even if you are not a lover of spice, add just the tiniest bit to the recipes that call for it; a little will go a long way in balancing the dish.

Temperature is the first sensation that the mouth senses. The temperature of our food affects our taste buds and influences the taste of the dish. A cold bean soup will not have the same flavor as a piping hot soup. The Pho Bowl with Seitan (page 136) is traditionally served extremely hot, and it actually tastes best that way. I've varied the temperatures of different components of some of these recipes to enhance the overall dining experience. Some salads, such as the Pad Prik King Tofu Salad Bowl (page 122) and the Vegan Chef's Salad Bowl (page 119), offer both a hot component and a cold component. Each enhances the flavor of the other because of the temperature variation.

When all the taste components of a dish—sweetness, saltiness, sourness, bitterness, umami, piquancy, and temperature—are in balance, a perfectly seasoned bowl is achieved. A dressing, for example, might be highly acidic on its own, but in combination with the entire bowl, the flavors come together in harmony. And that is the goal of these bowls: to unite otherwise seemingly divided ingredients into a meal of delicious unity.

getting started

Our lives are busy and getting busier, so putting food on the table in a timely manner is important to all of us. But serving delicious, well-balanced food that is varied and full of great flavors can add its own challenges. That's why this book is filled with a variety of recipes from around the world served in the convenience of a bowl. Most can be prepared in around 30 minutes.

This is not one-pot cooking! Even though the recipes are designed to be eaten in a single bowl, this is not "one-pot" cooking. To ensure that multiple components of a dish are ready at about the same time, you need to cook in more than a couple of pots. I hear you asking, "What about the clean up?" I've done the math, and it comes down to less time overall in the kitchen. If you use an additional pot to cook meals faster, you are out of the cooking phase 15 minutes earlier, and washing that extra pot takes just 2 minutes. Using an additional pot means that you leave the kitchen 13 minutes sooner.

Mise en place: "Mise en place" means "put in place," which means to prepare everything beforehand: measure, wash, and chop ingredients and only afterward get to the business of cooking. While most experienced cooks work best utilizing this method, the good news is that mise en place is optional when preparing recipes from this book. In fact, these recipes were created using no mise en place at all and washing and chopping ingredients as you go along.

kids in the kitchen

Although limiting distractions will help you keep focus on the recipe, if you have children who like to help out in the kitchen, tack on an extra 30 minutes to the cooking time and enjoy the shared moments.

Doubling and halving recipes: While it might seem that halving recipes might also halve the cooking time, be aware that halving recipes decreases your overall time in the kitchen by only a few minutes (around 5 to 8 minutes). However, doubling recipes (such as when cooking for a large group) will increase the overall time in the kitchen by up to 20 minutes.

A little spice is nice: Most of these recipes contain some heat, either via extra cracked black pepper, red pepper flakes, fresh chiles, or hot sauce. Feel free to adjust the heat level to your taste, but don't completely omit it, as the tiniest bit of heat adds balance.

time-saving tips for cooking

These are the steps I follow when preparing bowl recipes. The techniques will help you get dinner on the table faster than you may think possible. Utilizing them will shorten the time you spend in the kitchen and get you cooking with confidence.

Read your recipe: Twice. First, read the recipe to get a cursory idea of what to expect. Second, read the recipe while you mentally prepare the meal, paying attention to details. The recipe steps are written in the order that they should be accomplished; however, many of them include hands-off cooking time. For example, it takes about 20 minutes to cook pasta from the moment you put the pot of water on. While the water comes to a boil, you can begin making the sauce, and while the pasta actually cooks, you can be finishing the sauce.

Scan the recipe and assemble all needed equipment: Place your pots and pans on the stove. Pull out peelers, knives, strainers, blenders, and so on. You will not have the time to assemble a food processor while cooking, so do it now.

Pull out all obscure ingredients: We all do this: we know we have cornstarch in the pantry, but when it comes time to cook, we don't want to spend three minutes hunting for it. Or we know there is a bulb of fennel in the fridge, but when it comes time to shave it, the fennel is nowhere to be found, possibly tucked under the chard in the bottom drawer. It happens all the time, but when cooking these recipes quickly, you have no time to search for ingredients, so get them out ahead of time.

Knife skills: Using the right tool for the right job makes cooking much easier, but knowing how to use it is just as important. An easy way to increase your knife skills is through online videos. Cooking schools offer numerous professional online lessons for free! After that, becoming proficient is just a matter of practice.

Size matters: How big or small you chop your ingredients matters because smaller pieces cook faster. Similarly, same-size pieces cook evenly and finish cooking at the same time. For example, if you cut potatoes into 1/2-inch cubes, all the potato pieces will cook in about 13 minutes. However, the density of different vegetables also determines the amount of cooking time needed. For example, 1/2-inch cubes of zucchini will cook faster than the same size potato cubes. Size also mat-

preheat your pans

Don't be stuck with a bowl full of chopped onions under your nose while waiting for your pan to preheat. It is especially important to preheat cast iron pans, because they take about 4 minutes to heat up. Preheat cast iron pans early and preheat stainless steel pans a bit before you are done chopping whatever will need to go into them.

ters because it makes the food more pleasant to eat. Bowl recipes seldom need both a knife and a fork to eat, so cutting ingredients into bite-sized pieces is important. These recipes are specific regarding the size the vegetables should be cut to, thus ensuring that cooking time is quick and accurate. I keep a kitchen ruler handy, but with practice it becomes easy to judge a given length.

Make haste: You can cook these recipes in around 30 minutes, including chopping and measuring, but you will need to move quickly. Pretend you're a line cook and waste no time. Every minute counts.

Space: Chopping multiple ingredients on a small cutting board is not just frustrating, it slows you down. Have a large, clear work space ready before you cook; you will be amazed at the difference it makes. You will be able to chop various ingredients, keeping them separate and ready at the same time that you are actively cooking. Make sure your cutting board is stable and not sliding around while you are chopping. To increase traction, place a thin kitchen towel under it. Not only does this create a more stable cutting board that is efficient to use, it is also safer.

Use your senses: Listening to your pot of water will let you know when it is boiling, especially if the pot has a lid, since the lid will rattle. The sound of your onions cooking will let you know if you need to add a splash of broth to prevent burning, as the sizzling will slow down from lack of moisture. Subtle scents will alert you when nuts are toasted, when chiles are cooked, and when garlic is golden. Use as many of your senses as you can to be aware of different stages of cooking.

Look for the "Quick Tips" bowl icon (opposite): If you are prepared to cook your meal in around 30 minutes, adhere to the above suggestions and follow the Quick Tips for each recipe. They tell you right off what to get started first, such as boiling water for pasta or nuts and what is best prepped when, such as chopping your pepper while your onions are cooking. The Quick Tips assume that you have assembled all ingredients and equipment beforehand and that you cover your pot when bringing water (or broth) to a boil.

kitchen equipment

Below are tips about equipment that I find helpful for getting dinner on the table quickly.

Each piece of equipment has a permanent spot in my kitchen and I know exactly where it is even though it is put away in a drawer or on a shelf. For example, I have my whisks and spatulas on the counter near the stove and my bowls under the island where I do all my prep work. I also have a large, clear work surface that is safe for cutting and large enough to hold most of the recipe ingredients. Organize your standard setup as your own space allows. Here is my list of essential equipment and tools:

Blenders: small blender: These are more commonly known as Magic Bullet or personal blenders. These blenders are fantastic for blending small amounts of sauces and purées. **high-speed blender:** These are great for creating ultra-smooth sauces and purées. Popular brands are Vitamix and Blendtec. **stick blender:** These immersion blenders are a dream to use right inside pots and pans to blend large quantities of liquid.

Cake pans: round or square cake pans are lightweight pans and good for marinating ingredients because of their large, flat surface area and high sides. They also make great "bowls" for transferring ingredients from prep to pot.

Citrus reamer

Food processor: These machines make short work of finely mincing vegetables and making pestos, among other applications.

Grill pan: I use a cast iron 10-inch diameter grill pan. These pans need about 5 minutes to preheat properly. I do not recommend smoking in nonstick grill pans.

Knives: a very sharp 6-inch chef's knife is essential. I also use a good sharp paring knife

Lids for pots, pans, and skillets: Cookware lids not only speed up heating large amounts of liquid but also help caramelize onions faster and retain more flavor of the ingredients. If you have a skillet that does not have a lid, use a sheet of heavy-duty aluminum foil.

Mixing bowls: large for combining ingredients; medium and small for transferring chopped ingredients

Measuring cups (dry and liquid) and **measuring spoons**

Mandoline: Japanese V mandolines are probably the best for cutting ingredients into a variety of thicknesses, including paper-thin slices.

Pots and pans: I use three different sizes of pots: small saucepan (1 1/2 quarts), medium saucepan (3 quarts), and large pot (6 to 7 quarts).

Salad spinner

Skillet: I use a cast iron 12-inch diameter skillet. Cast iron needs to be preheated before using.

Spatula and wooden spoons

Vegetable peeler

recipe flexibility

low-oil or no-oil cooking: Recipes that call for 2 tablespoons of oil or less can easily be cooked with no oil, if desired, especially where the ingredient is sautéed. Instead of using oil, cook in an equal amount of vegetable broth. Using water brings no flavor to the dish, so sautéing with broth is a better option. Add a few splashes of broth as the pan or skillet dries out. Repeat as needed until the ingredient is cooked.

store-bought protein ingredients: Using commercial store-bought ingredients in some of these bowl recipes when needed is a great option. Vegan sausages, the Beyond Meat line of products, and other vegan proteins can provide an even quicker way to get dinner ready fast. Use the different products as you deem appropriate, especially in lieu of tempeh or seitan.

convenient recipe notations

The recipes in this book come with helpful notations designed to help you manage your food sensitivities, save time, and make easy ingredient substitutions.

GF (Gluten Free): These recipes are gluten-free with no substitution required.

GFO (Gluten-Free Option): These recipes are gluten-free with the indicated modifications.

SF (Soy Free): These recipes are soy-free with no substitution required.

SFO (Soy-Free Option): These recipes are soy-free with the indicated modifications.

Substitutions: The recipes also indicate ingredient substitutions where appropriate and possible.

 Quick Tips: Most recipes include Quick Tips to help you get your meal on the table in no time. Most people these days thrive on multitasking, and these tips help streamline kitchen prep with multitasking.

two | just-in-case basics

To make your weeknight meals a snap, I recommend using convenient store-bought ingredients wherever my recipes give the option. However, I recognize that many of us either do not have certain ingredients on hand, may have difficulty locating them where we live, or prefer to make our own. In those instances, these few basic recipes will augment the others in this book. You do not need to make these recipes in order to successfully create these dishes; they are supplemental recipes in case you need them or want to make them from scratch. I happen to love the Slow-Simmered Seitan and the Whole-Wheat Parker House Rolls, which are a great addition to meals, among other recipes in this chapter. Sometimes homemade really is superior, even when a convenient store-bought ingredient is readily available.

easy vegetable broth

MAKES 8 TO 9 CUPS | GF, SF

While it is quick and easy to purchase vegetable broth, this recipe is ready in about forty-five minutes and takes very little effort. It is a low-sodium broth that's suitable for use in any of the recipes in this book. The mushroom stems are optional but recommended. I save all my mushroom stems and keep them stored in an airtight container in the freezer to make this broth. I do the same with parsley stems.

2 teaspoons olive oil

2 medium onions, coarsely chopped

8 garlic cloves

10 cups water

6 medium carrots, coarsely chopped

6 celery ribs, coarsely chopped

1 small bell pepper, coarsely chopped (optional)

1/4 cup sun-dried tomatoes

1 cup mushroom stems (optional)

1 teaspoon fresh or dried thyme

1 teaspoon sea salt

1/2 teaspoon black pepper

2 bay leaves

1 cup coarsely chopped parsley stems

Heat the oil in a large pot over medium-high heat. Add the onion and garlic, cover, and cook until golden, stirring occasionally, about 8 minutes.

Stir in the water, carrot, celery, bell pepper, tomato, mushroom stems, if using, thyme, salt, pepper, and bay leaves. Bring to boil and reduce the heat to medium. Cook until the carrots are tender and the broth is well flavored, about 25 minutes.

Mash the vegetables with a potato masher, add the parsley and continue to cook for an additional 10 minutes.

Strain the broth into a large bowl using a colander. Mash the vegetables in the colander to release as much liquid as possible. Discard or compost the vegetables. Strain the broth using a fine mesh strainer. Store the broth in airtight containers for up to 7 days in the refrigerator or up to 6 months in the freezer.

cashew sour cream sauce

MAKES ABOUT 2/3 CUP | SF, GF

This sour cream sauce is made with cashews and almond milk. It is both soy-free and gluten-free and can be used in any recipe calling for sour cream.

1/3 cup raw cashew pieces

1/4 cup unsweetened plain unsweetened almond milk

1 tablespoon fresh lemon juice

1/2 teaspoon sea salt

Combine the cashews with enough water to cover in a small saucepan. Cover, bring to boil and cook for 5 minutes. Set aside for 5 minutes, then drain and rinse. Transfer the cashews to a small blender. Add the milk, lemon juice, and salt. Blend until it is as smooth as possible. If not using right away, transfer to an airtight container and keep refrigerated.

slow-simmered seitan

This seitan is semi-firm with an earthy flavor. It is fit for grilling, sautéing, and simmering in any of the recipes in this book. Although it has a distinctive flavor, it does not overpower any of the other components of the recipes. Seitan freezes very well in airtight containers, frozen with or without the cooking broth. In addition, the cooking broth can be reused for another batch of seitan or used as broth in other dishes.

MUSHROOMS
    1 cup vegetable broth
    1/2 ounce dried porcini mushrooms

VEGETABLES
    2 teaspoons plus 1 tablespoon grapeseed oil,
        divided
    1 cup finely chopped onion
    2 garlic cloves, crushed
    1/4 cup reduced-sodium tamari
    1 teaspoon smoked paprika
    1 teaspoon sea salt

SEITAN
    2 cups vital wheat gluten, stirred before measuring
    1 tablespoon whole-wheat flour
    8 cups vegetable broth

SOY-FREE OPTION: Substitute coconut aminos for the tamari, reduce the porcinis to 1/4 ounce and add 1/2 ounce sun-dried tomatoes with the porcinis to the vegetable broth.

SLOW COOKER: Pour all the broth into a slow cooker. Prepare the gluten slices in the same way as for baking. Place the gluten slices into the broth. Cover and cook on High for 3 hours or on Low for 8 hours, or until the seitan is firm to the touch.

MUSHROOMS: Heat the broth in a small saucepan over high heat. Bring to boil, add the porcini, cover, reduce to simmer, and cook for 3 minutes. Remove from heat and set aside for 10 minutes to soften. Drain the porcini, reserve the broth, and rinse the mushrooms. Set aside. Strain the broth using a coffee filter or reusable tea bag. Set aside.

VEGETABLES: Heat 2 teaspoons oil in a medium skillet over medium heat. Add the onion and garlic, cover and cook until caramelized, about 10 minutes. Stir occasionally, adding 2 to 3 tablespoons water as needed to prevent the onions from burning. In a blender, combine the tamari, paprika, salt, reserved porcinis and porcini liquid, onion mixture, and the remaining 1 tablespoon oil and blend until smooth. Set aside.

SEITAN: Combine the vital wheat gluten and whole-wheat flour in a large bowl and mix well. Add the blended broth, mix well and knead until smooth, about 5 minutes. If all the flour is not absorbed, add a splash of broth and knead again.

Cook using the oven method (below) or the slow cooker method (opposite).

OVEN: Heat the oven to 270°F (no need to preheat).Divide the broth between two 9 x 13-inch baking dishes. Shape the gluten into a log about 8 inches long. Cut off a thin slice, about 1/4 inch thick, and press it into a very thin piece on your work surface, using the palm of your hand. Dampen your work surface to prevent sticking. Place the gluten slice into the broth in the prepared dishes. Repeat with the remaining gluten, overlapping as needed. Cover the baking dishes tightly with aluminum foil. Bake for 2 hours. Cool completely before using in recipes.

chapatis

Chapatis, the everyday Indian flatbread (also known as roti), are soft and pliable. They are made of whole-wheat flour and are delicious with any of the Indian recipes in this book. Since they are technically tortillas, they are also great when you are craving a flour tortilla. Spread the chapatis with vegan butter, if desired.

2 cups whole-wheat flour
1 teaspoon sea salt
2 tablespoons grapeseed oil
3/4 to 1 cup hot water
Vegan butter (optional)

Combine the flour and salt in a medium bowl. Add the oil and mix. Add the water 1/4 cup at a time, until a soft, slightly sticky dough forms, kneading the dough as you add the water. Knead for 3 minutes.

Dust the dough with flour if it is too sticky and knead lightly. Cover and set aside for 20 minutes to rest.

Preheat a tawa or large cast iron skillet over medium heat. Divide the dough into 8 equal pieces. Shape each piece into a ball and flatten. Dip the disk in flour and, using a gentle hand, roll it out to 7 inches, about 1/16-inch thick.

Cook the chapati on the preheated skillet for 15 seconds, or until spots form on the bottom of the chapati. Flip and cook on the other side for 45 seconds. Remove the tawa or skillet and flip the chapati directly over the flame or burner. Move the chapati around until it puffs up. Transfer to a plate and spread with butter, if desired. Serve immediately or keep warm between layers of kitchen towels or in a tortilla warmer.

wine substitute

Some recipes call for red or white wine. Wines have a distinct tannic quality that lends an important flavor profile to recipes. Some people either cannot find vegan wines or prefer not to cook with them. If you choose to omit wine from your cooking, use this substitute:

1/2 cup sun-dried tomatoes
1 cup hot vegetable broth

Combine the sun-dried tomatoes and hot broth in a heatproof bowl. Set aside for at least 30 minutes to rehydrate and infuse the broth with the tomato flavor. Drain and squeeze the tomatoes of their liquid. Use the liquid in equal ratio to the wine called for in the recipes. (Save the squeezed tomatoes for another use.) Makes about 3/4 cup.

corn tortillas

MAKES 12 (5-INCH) TORTILLAS | GF, SF

Homemade corn tortillas are worlds apart from their store-bought counterparts. In addition to being quite delicious, these tortillas will not crack when folded. The secret: press the tortillas into a thin disk and keep them warm between towels. Keeping them warm will lightly steam them and keep them soft and flexible.

2 cups masa harina
1/2 teaspoon sea salt
1 1/2 cups hot water

Combine the masa harina and salt in a medium bowl. Add the water and stir together with a spoon. When cool enough to handle, mix the dough lightly with your hand and form into a ball. Cover and set aside for 20 minutes to rest.

Preheat a griddle or large cast iron skillet over medium-high heat. Divide the dough into 12 equal pieces. Prepare a tortilla press by lining it with 16x8-inch waxed paper folded in half. Shape a piece of dough into a ball and flatten between your hands. Place the disk between the waxed paper, slightly off-center. Press the disk into a thin tortilla. Repeat the procedure until the tortilla is about 1/16-inch thick.

Alternatively, place the disk between the waxed paper and press down on the disk using a round cake pan or round pie pan with a flat bottom. Lift the waxed paper off both the top and bottom of the tortilla and repeat the procedure until your tortilla is about 1/16-inch thick.

Cook the tortilla on the preheated griddle for 30 seconds, flip, cook for another 30 seconds. Flip one more time and cook for an additional 20 seconds. Keep warm between layers of kitchen towels or in a tortilla warmer.

red curry paste

MAKES ABOUT 1 1/4 CUPS | GF, SF

Making your own red curry paste is a simple process that gives great returns on time invested. The flavor beats a jar of store-bought any day. I use two kinds of red chiles, one mild and one hot, but you can use any dried red chiles you can find. Just be aware that the heat of the chiles you use will determine the heat level of your paste. As written, this is a very mild curry paste. To increase the heat, reduce the number of Anaheim chiles, also known as California chiles, to 6 and increase the number of hot red chiles to 20 or more.

10 dried Anaheim chiles

2 small dried red hot chiles, any kind

1/4 cup coarsely chopped galangal or ginger

1/4 cup coarsely chopped garlic

1 small red onion, coarsely chopped

2 stalks lemongrass (see Note)

2 tablespoons minced kaffir lime leaves or lime zest

1 teaspoon salt

2 tablespoons water

NOTE: To prepare lemongrass, cut off the bottom 2 inches of the stalk. Cut off the top 4 to 6 inches of the papery stalk. Remove and discard 2 or 3 tough outer leaves. Cut the remaining stalk into 2 pieces, each about 3 inches long. Using a rolling pin, smash the pieces to release the flavor and essential oil. Cut the stalks into small pieces.

Remove the stems and most of the seeds from the chiles. Toast the chiles in a large dry skillet over medium heat until they darken, about 2 minutes. Transfer the chiles to a large bowl and add enough hot water to cover. Set aside for 10 minutes to soften.

Drain the chiles and add them to a food processor. Add the galangal, garlic, onion, lemongrass, lime, and salt. Process until finely ground. Add the 2 tablespoons fresh water and process until smooth as possible, about 2 minutes.

Transfer the paste to an airtight container. The paste will keep for up to 3 weeks. Do not freeze the paste, as most of the pungency will be lost.

QUICK TIPS: Chop the veggies while the chiles soak.

chipotle purée

MAKES ABOUT 1 CUP | SF, GF

Keep some chipotle purée on hand to add a smoky heat to any dish.

1 (7-ounce) can chipotle chiles in adobo sauce

Transfer the entire contents of the can of chipotles, including the sauce, to a small blender and blend until smooth. Store the purée in an airtight container in the refrigerator for up to two months.

whole-wheat parker house rolls

MAKES 12 ROLLS | SF

Parker House Rolls were invented at the Omni Parker House Hotel in Boston in the late 1800s. The rolls are fluffy, buttery, sweet and crisp on the outside. This is my whole-wheat version using olive oil. The variation at the end of the recipe uses vegan butter. The original shape of the rolls was round, but that makes for a lot of leftover dough and much more work. This version produces rectangular rolls.

1 cup plus 2 tablespoons unsweetened plain
   nondairy milk

1/4 cup natural sugar

3 tablespoons olive oil, divided

2 teaspoons active dry yeast

2 3/4 cups whole-wheat flour

1/4 cup vital wheat gluten

1 1/4 teaspoons sea salt

VARIATION: Buttered Parker House Rolls. Substitute 6 tablespoons vegan butter for the olive oil. Melt 4 tablespoons butter, add 1 cup of nondairy milk and warm to 100°F. Reduce the salt to 1 teaspoon. Melt the remaining 2 tablespoons vegan butter. Brush the baking pan lightly with the butter and brush the remaining butter over the rolled-out dough before folding the pieces in half.

Heat the milk and sugar in small saucepan over medium heat. Warm the mixture to around 100°F or warm to the touch. Stir in 1 tablespoon oil and the yeast and set aside to bloom, about 5 minutes. Combine the flour, vital wheat gluten, and salt in a medium bowl, mixing well, and set aside.

Transfer the yeast mixture to a stand mixer and whisk in half of the flour mixture using a hand whisk. Add the rest of the flour mixture and knead with the dough hook until smooth, about 6 minutes, scraping the sides as needed. The dough will be very sticky, but avoid adding more flour.

Add 1 tablespoon oil to a clean bowl. Using oiled hands or spatula, transfer the dough to the bowl. Cover with plastic wrap and set aside in a warm spot to double in size, about 1 hour. When you can poke the dough with a finger and leave a deep indentation, the dough is ready.

Transfer the dough to a dry work surface. Because the dough is oiled, there is no need for additional flour. Roll or press the dough into a rectangle about 7 x 11-inches x 1/2-inch thick. Cut the dough lengthwise into four pieces, 11 inches long. Cut the dough again width-wise into 3 pieces.

Prepare a 9 x 9-inch metal baking pan (brownie pans work well) by greasing the pan with 1 tablespoon oil. Fold each piece of dough in half into a 2- x 2-inch square. Fit the dough pieces into the pan. Brush the rolls with any remaining oil left in the proofing bowl, cover with the plastic wrap and set aside to double, about 30 minutes.

Place a pie pan filled with 1 cup of water on the bottom rack of the oven. Preheat the oven to 375°F. Remove the wrap gently from the rolls and bake until golden brown, 18 to 20 minutes. Brush with additional olive oil if desired and allow to cool slightly. Transfer the rolls to a warming basket and enjoy.

30-minute brown rice

MAKES ABOUT 3 CUPS | GF, SF

Long-grain brown rice can be prepared in a fraction of the normal time using this cooking method. Cooking the rice in enough water to keep the grains in constant motion, while continually surrounding each grain with water, helps the rice to cook in around 20 minutes. Since rice can absorb more or less water, depending on the brand and strain, you should begin checking for doneness after 15 minutes of cooking. Do not skip the steaming step, which will ensure that your rice is fluffy.

6 cups water

1 teaspoon sea salt

1 1/2 cups long-grain brown rice

Combine the water, salt, and brown rice in a large pot over high heat. Bring the water to boil and reduce to a strong simmer over medium heat. Cook the rice until tender. Begin testing for doneness after 15 minutes.

Drain the rice using a fine mesh strainer and return the rice to the pot. Cover the pot with a kitchen towel and set aside to steam for 5 minutes. Fluff the rice and serve.

perfect quinoa

MAKES ABOUT 4 CUPS | GF, SF

Quinoa should be fluffy, like well-cooked long grain rice, but still tender. A good indication that your quinoa is cooked is when the tail of the quinoa separates from the body. Cooking the quinoa in considerably less liquid than is typically called for will make your quinoa tender and fluffy, not bogged down with liquid.

1 1/2 cups vegetable broth

1/2 teaspoon sea salt

1 cup quinoa, well rinsed

Heat the broth and salt in a small saucepan over high heat. After rinsing the quinoa in a very fine mesh strainer until the water runs clear, add to the broth and bring to a boil. Cover, reduce the heat to simmer over medium-low heat and cook for 15 minutes.

Remove the quinoa from the heat and set aside, covered, to steam for 10 minutes. Fluff with a fork before serving.

seitan gyro bowl (page 36)

three | grain bowls

Grains take center stage in many cultures, and rice, wheat, and corn play an important role in my bowl dishes as well. In this chapter, grains are the star, while the other plant-based ingredients are cast in supporting roles. The two risotto recipes are perfect examples, with creamy rice enhanced by a variety of vegetables, beans, and seasonings to create delicious meals in a bowl. I also include my spin on an ancient Hungarian dish known as sólet, using farro instead of the traditional barley. Other wonderful and nutritious meals in this chapter embrace quinoa, polenta, and freekeh.

paella bowl

SERVES 4 TO 6 | GF, SF

The saffron threads are responsible for the beautiful orange-yellow color of this dish. Once the rice and broth are added, the dish is no longer stirred. It cooks uncovered while the rice absorbs the broth. As the rice cooks, it develops a flavorful crust on the bottom of the pan called *socarrat* – a welcome result of not stirring the rice. Using a nonstick pan will prevent the socarrat from forming, but the dish will still taste great.

BROTH

3 1/2 cups vegetable broth

2 teaspoons smoked paprika

1 teaspoon sea salt

1/4 teaspoon saffron threads

SAUTÉ

3 tablespoons olive oil

5 artichoke hearts, quartered

1 medium yellow squash or zucchini, halved lengthwise and cut into 1/4-inch slices

1 small red bell pepper, coarsely chopped

1 small Roma tomato, coarsely chopped

4 garlic cloves, minced

4 ounces green beans, trimmed and cut into 2-inch pieces

2 cups frozen lima beans or edamame, thawed

1 cup paella or Arborio rice

GARNISH

1/2 cup green peas, thawed if frozen

1 jarred roasted red pepper, cut into 1/2-inch strips

1/4 cup minced parsley

Lemon slices

BROTH: Heat the broth, paprika, salt, and saffron in a medium saucepan over high heat. Bring to boil, reduce to simmer. Cover and keep warm over low heat.

SAUTÉ: Heat the oil in a 12-inch skillet over medium-high heat. Add the artichoke and squash and cook until golden brown, about 4 minutes. Transfer to a medium bowl. Add the bell pepper, tomato, and garlic. Cook, stirring occasionally, until the tomatoes break down, about 5 minutes. Add the green beans and lima beans. Add the rice, spreading it evenly over the vegetables. Add the broth, taking care not to disturb the rice too much, but ensuring that the rice is submerged in the broth. Reduce the heat to medium and cook until the rice is al dente, about 14 minutes.

Arrange the squash and artichoke hearts on the paella and continue to cook until the rice is tender and the broth is absorbed, about 4 minutes longer.

GARNISH: Scatter the peas over the paella, arrange the strips of pepper on top of the paella and sprinkle with the parsley. Remove from the heat, cover and set aside for 5 minutes before serving. Serve in bowls with lemon slices.

QUICK TIPS: Preheat the skillet while you chop the artichokes and squash. Chop the bell pepper, tomato, and garlic while the artichoke and squash cook. Chop the green beans while the bell pepper cooks.

roasted zucchini and mushroom pilaf bowl

SERVES 4 | GFO, SF

It is no surprise that I love to roast vegetables; it always seems to bring out the best in produce. In this recipe, zucchini and mushrooms are roasted to perfection and stirred into a quinoa pilaf that is accented with scallions and arugula.

ROAST

- 2 tablespoons olive oil
- 1/2 teaspoon sea salt
- 4 garlic cloves, minced
- 8 ounces cremini or button mushrooms, wiped clean and quartered
- 2 medium zucchini, quartered and cut into 3/4-inch slices
- 1 cup corn kernels, thawed and drained if frozen

QUINOA

- 1 1/4 cups vegetable broth
- 1/2 teaspoon sea salt
- 1 cup quinoa, well rinsed
- 2 garlic cloves, crushed

PASTA

- 1 tablespoon olive oil
- 1/2 cup orzo
- 2 cups water
- 1/4 teaspoon sea salt

GREENS

- 3 cups baby arugula or watercress
- 2 scallions, minced
- 1/2 to 1 serrano chile, minced
- 1 tablespoon fresh lemon juice

GLUTEN-FREE OPTION: Substitute 1/4 cup long grain rice for the orzo. Cook until tender, about 10 minutes for white rice and 20 minutes for brown rice.

ROAST: Preheat the oven to 450°F. Combine the oil, salt and garlic on a baking sheet. Add the mushroom, zucchini, and corn. Mix well and bake until tender and roasted, about 20 minutes, stirring midway through cooking time. If you have more time, roast until the corn is golden, an additional 5 to 10 minutes. Keep warm.

QUINOA: Heat the broth, salt, quinoa and garlic in a large pot. Cover, bring to boil over high heat, reduce to medium-low heat and cook for 15 minutes. Remove from heat and set aside for 10 minutes to steam. Fluff with fork and set aside.

PASTA: Heat the oil in a medium saucepan over medium-high heat. Add the orzo and cook, stirring frequently, until golden brown. Add the water and salt and bring to boil. Reduce to simmer and cook until tender, 7 to 9 minutes. Drain and set aside.

GREENS: Add the orzo to the cooked quinoa. Add the roasted vegetables to the quinoa. Add the arugula, scallions, serrano and lemon juice. Stir well, taste and adjust seasoning with salt and black pepper.

QUICK TIPS: Begin by preheating the oven to 450°F, then heat the broth for the quinoa in a covered saucepan.

sólet bowl

SERVES 4 TO 6 | GFO, SF

This hearty ancient Hungarian dish is traditionally an overnight-cooked meal of barley, beans, paprika, and onions, occasionally with the addition of meat. I grew up eating sólet and wanted to recreate its slow-cooked flavors but have the dish ready for the table in much less time. The flavors here are just as great as in the original. A few minutes in the oven does wonders for this recipe.

BROTH

- 4 cups vegetable broth
- 4 large or 6 small black cardamom pods
- 1 tablespoon Hungarian paprika
- 1 teaspoon sea salt
- 1 cup pearled farro, well rinsed
- 2 cups cooked kidney or pinto beans
- 4 garlic cloves, crushed
- 12 ounces russet potatoes, peeled and cut into 1-inch cubes
- 2 large carrots, cut into 1/2-inch rounds

LECSÓ

- 1 teaspoon olive oil
- 1 large onion, cut into 1/8 inch thick slices
- 1/4 cup vegetable broth, divided
- 1 medium red or green bell pepper, coarsely chopped
- 2 medium Roma tomatoes, coarsely chopped
- 1/2 teaspoon sea salt
- 2 teaspoons whole-wheat pastry flour or all-purpose flour

GARNISH

- 2 tablespoons olive oil
- Kosher or dill pickles, as needed

SUBSTITUTION: Substitute 1 teaspoon liquid smoke for the black cardamom. Substitute pearled barley, soaked overnight, for the farro.

GLUTEN-FREE OPTION: Substitute brown rice for the farro and cook until tender. Omit the whole-wheat pastry flour.

BROTH: Combine the broth, cardamom, paprika, salt, farro, beans, garlic, potatoes and carrot in a large oven-safe pot over high heat. Cover, bring to boil and reduce to a strong simmer over medium heat. Cook for 10 minutes. Preheat the oven to 450°F. Uncover the pot and continue to cook for an additional 10 minutes or until the farro is al dente.

LECSÓ: Heat the oil in a large skillet over medium heat. Add the onion, cover and cook until the onion softens, about 4 minutes, stirring occasionally. Add 2 tablespoons of broth and the bell pepper. Cover and cook until the bell pepper softens, about 4 more minutes, stirring occasionally. Add the remaining 2 tablespoons broth and the tomatoes. Cook, uncovered, until the tomatoes break down, about 4 more minutes.

Add the flour to the lecsó and mix well. Cook 1 minute and add the lecsó to the simmering broth. Mix well and cook until thickened, about 1 minute.

GARNISH: Drizzle the oil over the top of the sólet. Transfer the pot to the preheated oven and bake for 10 minutes. Serve with the pickles.

QUICK TIPS: Begin by heating the broth with the farro and cardamom, then add the other ingredients. Prepare the onions before you chop the potato and carrot. Remember to preheat the oven about 10 minutes into the cooking time.

southern beans and grits bowl with collards

SERVES 4 | GF, SFO

Southern beans and grits are a simple dish, often served with sausage. Using carrots adds texture to the dish, but using vegan sausage instead of, or with, the carrots is equally delicious. The beans and gravy are lightly smoky and pair wonderfully with the creamy grits.

BROTH

- 2 cups vegetable broth
- 4 black cardamom pods
- 1/4 cup sun-dried tomatoes

GRITS

- 2 1/2 cups vegetable broth
- 1/2 teaspoon sea salt
- 1 1/4 cups medium-ground corn grits, cornmeal, or polenta (do not use instant)
- 1 1/2 cups unsweetened plain nondairy milk, divided
- 1 tablespoon white miso
- 1 tablespoon olive oil
- Sea salt and black pepper

COLLARDS

- 8 ounces collard greens, stemmed and chopped
- 1/2 teaspoon sea salt
- 1 tablespoon olive oil
- 3 large carrots, cut into 3/4-inch rounds

SAUTÉ

- 1 teaspoon toasted sesame oil
- 4 garlic cloves, minced
- 2 tablespoons tomato paste
- 4 cups cooked kidney beans
- 1 teaspoon dried thyme
- 1/2 teaspoon dried oregano
- 2 scallions, minced

SOY-FREE OPTION: Substitute chickpea miso for the white miso.

SUBSTITUTION: Replace the carrots with 3 vegan sausage links, cut into 1/2-inch rounds. Brown in the skillet and set aside to add to the sauté along with the cooked collards. Substitute 1 teaspoon liquid smoke for the cardamom.

BROTH: Combine the broth, cardamom, and tomatoes in a small saucepan. Bring to boil over high heat, reduce to simmer, cover and cook until needed. Strain the broth before using, discarding the cardamom. Mince the sun-dried tomatoes and return to the broth.

GRITS: Bring the broth and salt to a boil in a medium saucepan, covered, over high heat. Stir in the grits and simmer over medium heat until thick, 2 to 5 minutes. Stir in 1 cup of milk and simmer over low heat until the grits are tender, 10 to 15 minutes, partly covered. Stir in the remaining 1/2 cup of milk before serving if the grits are too thick. Stir in the miso and oil. Taste and season with salt and pepper. Set aside. Keep warm.

COLLARDS: Bring a medium saucepan of water to boil. Add the collards and salt and simmer over medium heat. Heat the oil in a large skillet over medium-high heat. Add the carrots and cook, stirring occasionally, until browned. Add the carrots to the collards and cook until tender, 8 to 10 minutes. Drain and set aside.

SAUTÉ: Add the sesame oil and the garlic to the large skillet. Cook, stirring constantly, until the garlic is golden, about 1 minute. Stir in the tomato paste and cook until darkened, about 30 seconds. Stir in the beans, thyme, and oregano. Stir in the broth with the sun-dried tomatoes. Cook for a few minutes to heat the beans and lightly mash with a potato masher. Stir in the drained collards and carrots. Cook until the sauce thickens and reduces by one-third. Season with salt and pepper. Serve the grits in bowls with the beans. Garnish with scallions.

sweet and spicy eggplant-zucchini bowl

SERVES 4 | GF

This recipe is a take on a popular Chinese restaurant dish. Instead of deep-frying the eggplant, I grill it and then toss it with a sweet and spicy sauce. I've added zucchini and cashews to boost the nutrition. If you have toasted cashews on hand, feel free to use them instead of toasting your own.

RICE

- 1 1/2 cups water
- 1 teaspoon sea salt
- 1 cup long-grain white rice

MARINADE

- 2 tablespoons vegetable broth
- 1 teaspoon grapeseed oil
- 1/2 teaspoon black pepper
- 2 medium zucchini, cut into 1-inch slices
- 1 medium eggplant, cut into 1-inch slices

SAUCE

- 6 tablespoons reduced-sodium tamari
- 1/4 cup vegetable broth
- 2 tablespoons sambal oelek
- 2 tablespoons rice vinegar
- 2 tablespoons natural brown sugar

NUTS

- 1 teaspoon grapeseed oil
- 1/2 cup cashew pieces

VEGETABLES

- 1 teaspoon grapeseed oil
- 2 celery ribs, cut into 1/4-inch slices
- 8 garlic cloves, minced
- 1 (1-inch) piece ginger, grated
- 4 scallions, cut into 2-inch pieces
- 1 tablespoon cornstarch mixed with 2 tablespoons vegetable broth

SUBSTITUTION: Substitute brown rice for the white rice—use the 30-Minute Brown Rice recipe (page 16).

RICE: Heat the water and salt in a small saucepan over high heat. Rinse the rice in two changes of fresh water and add to the pan. When the water is bubbling on the sides of the pan, cover and reduce the heat to low. Cook for 15 minutes. Remove from the heat and set aside for 10 minutes to steam. Fluff with a fork before serving.

MARINADE: Preheat a grill pan over medium heat. Combine the broth, oil, and pepper in a large bowl. Toss the zucchini slices with the marinade and grill the slices until almost tender, about 3 minutes per side. Transfer to a work surface and cut into bite-sized pieces and set aside.

Toss the eggplant slices with the remaining marinade and grill until almost tender, about 4 minutes per side. Turn the slices a quarter turn after 2 minutes to achieve a criss-cross pattern. This will help the eggplant cook but not burn. Transfer to a work surface and cut into bite-size pieces. Set aside.

SAUCE: Combine the tamari, broth, sambal oelek, vinegar, and sugar in a small bowl and set aside.

NUTS: Heat the oil in a large pot over medium heat. Stir in the cashews and cook until golden, 3 to 5 minutes. Remove from the pot and set aside.

VEGETABLES: Heat the oil in the large pot over medium-high heat. Stir in the celery and cook 1 minute. Stir in the garlic, ginger, and scallions and cook 1 minute. Reduce heat to medium and add the reserved eggplant, zucchini and sauce. Stir, cover and cook until the eggplant is tender, 3 to 5 minutes. Stir in the cornstarch mixture and cook just until thickened. Remove from heat and stir in the reserved cashews. Serve with the rice.

 QUICK TIPS: Begin by heating the water for the rice and heating the grill pan (takes about 4 minutes). Rinse the rice as the water heats. Add the eggplant to the marinade so it can soak it up for as long as possible.

spicy ginger polenta bowl
with bok choy and chickpeas

SERVES 2 TO 3 | GF, SFO

Polenta might not be the first grain-based dish you think of to season with ginger, but this easy and quick recipe is delicious. The ginger imparts its flavor to the polenta and the simple sauce complements the bok choy and chickpeas.

POLENTA

- 1 teaspoon grapeseed oil
- 3 garlic cloves, minced
- 1 1/2 cups vegetable broth
- 1 teaspoon grated ginger
- 1/4 to 1/2 teaspoons red pepper flakes
- 1/4 teaspoon sea salt
- 1/2 cup plus 2 tablespoons polenta
- 3/4 cup unsweetened plain nondairy milk, divided
- Sea salt and black pepper

CHICKPEAS

- 1 teaspoon toasted sesame oil
- 2 cups cooked chickpeas, patted dry

BOK CHOY

- 1 tablespoon grapeseed oil
- 1 teaspoon toasted sesame oil
- 10 ounces baby bok choy, halved lengthwise

SAUCE

- 1 teaspoon toasted sesame oil
- 4 garlic cloves, minced
- 1 teaspoon grated ginger
- 1/2 cup vegetable broth
- 2 tablespoons reduced-sodium tamari

SOY-FREE OPTION: Substitute coconut aminos and 1/8 teaspoon sea salt for the tamari.

POLENTA: Heat the oil over medium heat in a small saucepan. Stir in the garlic and cook until golden, about 1 minute. Stir in the broth, ginger, red pepper flakes, and salt. Increase heat to high and bring to boil, covered. Stir in the polenta with a whisk and simmer over medium-low heat until thickened, 2 to 5 minutes. Stir in 1/2 cup of milk and simmer over low heat until the polenta is tender, 10 to 15 minutes, partly covered. Remove from heat and stir in the remaining 1/4 cup of milk, if needed. Taste and adjust seasoning with salt and pepper. Keep warm.

CHICKPEAS: Heat the oil in a large skillet over medium-high heat. Add the chickpeas and season with salt. Cook until golden brown, about 5 minutes, stirring occasionally. Transfer to a small bowl and set aside.

BOK CHOY: Return the skillet to the heat and reduce the heat to medium. Add the oils to the hot skillet, then add the bok choy, cut side down, and cook until lightly charred and crisp-tender, 5 to 8 minutes. Remove the bok choy from the skillet and set aside on a work surface. Chop if desired.

SAUCE: Return the skillet to the stove over medium heat. Add the oil, then stir in the garlic and ginger. Cook until the garlic is golden. Carefully add the vegetable broth and tamari. Stir in the chickpeas and cook until the sauce reduces by one-quarter, about 4 minutes. To serve, spoon the polenta in bowls and top with the bok choy and chickpeas. Serve immediately.

QUICK TIPS: Mince the ginger for both the polenta and the sauce at the same time. Mince the garlic for both the polenta and the sauce at the same time; you will need 7 cloves. Clean and halve the bok choy while the chickpeas cook.

winter risotto bowl

SERVES 4 TO 6 | GF, SF

Butternut squash risotto is a classic Italian dish, but I amp up the nutrition and flavor with the addition of baby spinach and roasted chickpeas, always a favorite combination. Roasting the butternut squash brings out its lovely sweetness.

BROTH

- 6 cups vegetable broth
- 1 teaspoon dried sage
- 1 teaspoon sea salt

CHICKPEAS

- 2 cups cooked chickpeas
- 1 teaspoon olive oil
- 2 garlic cloves, minced
- 1/2 teaspoon sea salt

SQUASH

- 1 small (1 pound) butternut squash, peeled, seeded and cut into 1/2-inch dice
- 2 teaspoons olive oil
- 1/2 teaspoon sea salt
- 1/4 teaspoon cayenne

RICE

- 1 tablespoon olive oil
- 1 1/2 cups Arborio rice
- 1/2 cup dry white wine or dry vermouth
- 4 cups baby spinach

 QUICK TIPS: First, preheat the oven to 450°F, then heat the broth. Cut off both ends of the squash before peeling with a vegetable peeler. Use an ice cream scoop to scoop out the seeds of the squash.

BROTH: Heat the broth, sage and salt in a medium saucepan over high heat. Bring to boil, cover and reduce to simmer over medium-low heat until needed.

CHICKPEAS: Preheat the oven to 450°F. Combine the chickpeas, oil, garlic, and salt on a small baking sheet. Bake the chickpeas until golden, about 15 minutes, stirring midway through baking.

SQUASH: Combine the squash, oil, salt and cayenne on a separate small or medium baking sheet and bake until tender, about 20 minutes, stirring midway through the baking.

RICE: Heat the oil in a large pot over medium-high heat. Stir in the rice and cook until the rice is translucent around the edges, about 4 minutes. Stir in the wine and cook until evaporated. Reduce the heat to medium and add 2 cups broth mixture. Cook, stirring about every 2 minutes, until the broth is absorbed, 7 to 10 minutes. Stir in more broth mixture, 1/2 cup at a time, until the rice is tender, about 10 more minutes, using only as much broth as needed; it is likely you will need most of it. You will need to stir more frequently, about every minute, to prevent the rice from sticking to the pot. The risotto is done when the rice is tender and creamy but not mushy, and most of the broth in the large pot is absorbed. You should be able to scrape the bottom of the pot with a spatula and not have any broth covering the path for a few seconds.

ASSEMBLY: Stir in the roasted squash, chickpeas and baby spinach. Cook and stir until the spinach wilts and the squash is heated through, about 1 minute. Taste and adjust seasonings before serving.

tex-mex risotto bowl

SERVES 4 TO 6 | GF, SF

This risotto embraces the flavors of my husband's home state, Texas. It is delicious and easy to make. The chipotle purée adds a bit of smoky spice to the risotto, and the roasted corn makes for happy diners. Make sure to thaw and drain your corn well before roasting.

BROTH

6 cups light vegetable broth, if using strong broth, use 3 cups broth and 3 cups water

2 teaspoons Chipotle Purée (page 14)

2 teaspoons ground cumin

2 teaspoons dried oregano

2 teaspoons sea salt

RICE

1 tablespoon grapeseed oil

1 1/2 cups Arborio rice

3/4 cup dry vermouth or dry white wine

VEGETABLES

1 tablespoon grapeseed oil

1 medium onion, finely chopped

2 cups frozen corn kernels, rinsed to thaw, then drained

1 medium zucchini, cut into 1/2-inch dice

1 1/2 cups chopped ripe tomatoes

4 garlic cloves, minced

2 cups cooked black beans

2 to 3 teaspoons fresh lime juice

Black pepper

1/4 cup minced cilantro

 QUICK TIPS: Chop the onion while the rice is toasting. Chop the zucchini and garlic as the rice simmers during the first 10 minutes.

BROTH: Combine the broth, chipotle, cumin, oregano, and salt in a medium saucepan over high heat. Cover, bring to boil and reduce to simmer. Keep warm and use as needed.

RICE: Heat the oil in a large pot over medium-high heat. Stir in the rice and cook until the rice is translucent around the edges, about 4 minutes. Stir in the wine and cook until evaporated. Reduce the heat to medium and add 2 cups broth mixture. Cook, stirring frequently, until the broth is absorbed, 7 to 10 minutes.

Stir in more broth mixture, one half cup at a time, until the rice is tender, about 10 more minutes, using only as much broth as needed; it is likely you will need most of it. You will need to stir more frequently, about every minute, to prevent the rice from sticking to the pot. The risotto is done when the rice is tender and creamy, but not mushy, and most of the broth in the large pot is absorbed. You should be able to scrape the bottom of the pot with a spatula and not have any broth covering the path for a few seconds.

VEGETABLES: Heat the oil in a large skillet over medium-high heat. Stir in the onion and corn and cook until the corn is golden and roasted, about 10 minutes. Stir in the zucchini, tomato and garlic, cover and cook until the zucchini is almost tender. Add the zucchini mixture and the beans to the rice when the rice done and cook to heat through, about 1 minute. Remove the risotto from the heat and stir in the lime juice. Season with salt and pepper. Serve in bowls and garnish with the cilantro.

freekeh stir-fry bowl
with broccoli and shiitake

SERVES 4 | GFO, SFO

You'll be surprised by how beautifully freekeh stands in for rice in this twist on a traditional stir-fry. Freekeh, broccoli, and mushrooms bring on the protein; and the dish is quite pretty to boot.

FREEKEH

2 1/2 cups vegetable broth

1 cup cracked freekeh

2 garlic cloves, crushed

1 (1/2-inch) piece ginger, halved

1/2 teaspoon sea salt

STIR-FRY

1 tablespoon grapeseed oil

6 ounces shiitake mushrooms, wiped clean, stems removed, cut into 1/4-inch slices

1 pound broccoli, cut into florets and the stems peeled and sliced

1 medium red bell pepper, cut into 1/4-inch slices

2 scallions, cut into 1/4-inch slices on the diagonal

4 garlic cloves, minced

1 (8-ounce) can water chestnuts, rinsed and drained

1/2 cup raw hazelnuts or almonds, chopped

SAUCE

2 tablespoons reduced-sodium tamari

2 tablespoons fresh lemon juice

1 1/2 tablespoons toasted sesame oil

1/2 to 1 teaspoon red pepper flakes

Sea salt and black pepper

1 tablespoon toasted sesame seeds

GLUTEN-FREE OPTION: Use 3 cups of cooked and cooled brown rice instead of the freekeh. Omit the freekeh directions and add 1 teaspoon minced ginger with the scallions and garlic.

SOY-FREE OPTION: Substitute coconut aminos and 1/8 teaspoon sea salt for the tamari.

FREEKEH: Combine the broth, freekeh, garlic, ginger and salt in a medium saucepan over high heat. Cover, bring to boil, reduce to simmer over medium-low and cook until the freekeh is tender, about 15 minutes. Remove the ginger and discard. Set aside until needed.

STIR-FRY: Heat the oil until it shimmers in a large skillet or wok over medium-high heat. Add the mushrooms and cook, stirring constantly, until soft, about 2 minutes. Add the broccoli and cook until bright green, about 2 minutes. Add the bell pepper, scallions, garlic, water chestnuts and hazelnuts. Stir and cook until the peppers are softened, 2 to 3 minutes.

SAUCE: Add the cooked freekeh, along with any remaining broth, to the skillet. Add the tamari, lemon juice, oil and red pepper flakes. Stir well and cook until the sauce is evaporated, about 2 minutes. Season with salt and pepper. Serve in bowls garnished with the sesame seeds.

 QUICK TIPS: Heat the broth for the freekeh while you prepare the garlic and ginger. Chop and assemble all the ingredients for the stir-fry and sauce while the freekeh cooks. Once the freekeh is cooked, the stir-fry comes together fast.

SUBSTITUTION: Use 1 ounce of dried shiitake mushrooms instead of fresh. Reconstitute in boiling water for 15 minutes, gently squeeze of excess moisture, remove stems and slice.

thai panang curry bowl

SERVES 4 | GF, SFO

We have always loved panang curry, but even more so now that we make our own at home. This is such a simple recipe that it almost feels like cheating. In addition to being quick, this curry is super flexible; use any variety of vegetables that you please. If you are using store-bought curry paste, adjust the amount to taste and make sure there is no peanut butter in the paste, as this recipe already contains the nut butter.

QUINOA

- 1 cup quinoa, rinsed well
- 1 1/2 cups vegetable broth
- 1 garlic clove, crushed
- 1/4 teaspoon sea salt
- 1/2 cup green peas, thawed if frozen

CURRY

- 1 (13.5-ounce) can coconut milk, divided
- 3 tablespoons Red Curry Paste (page 14) or 1 to 2 tablespoons store-bought
- 2 tablespoons peanut butter
- 3 (2-lobed) kaffir lime leaves
- 2 tablespoons reduced-sodium tamari
- 1/4 to 1/2 cup water
- 5 cups coarsely chopped vegetables (carrot, winter squash, summer squash, green beans)
- 1 cup sliced red bell pepper
- Sea salt and black pepper
- 1/2 cup Thai basil or Genoese basil

SOY-FREE OPTION: Substitute coconut aminos and 1/8 teaspoon sea salt for the tamari.

QUINOA: Heat the quinoa, broth, garlic and salt in a small saucepan. Cover, bring to boil over high heat, reduce to medium-low heat, cover and cook for 15 minutes. Remove from heat and set aside for 10 minutes. Fluff with fork and add peas before serving.

CURRY: Heat 1/4 cup coconut milk in a large pot over medium heat. Add the curry paste and cook until the milk reduces a bit, about 1 minute. Add another 1/4 cup of the milk and the peanut butter and cook for another minute. Add the remaining milk, the lime leaves, tamari, and 1/4 cup of water. Add the tough vegetables (carrot, winter squash) and cook for 4 minutes. Add the soft vegetables (summer squash, green beans) and simmer over medium until the vegetables are tender. Add the bell pepper and cook until crisp tender, about 1 minute. Add more water if the curry is too dry. Season with salt and pepper. To serve, divide the curry and quinoa among 4 bowls. Garnish with the basil.

QUICK TIPS: Prepare the vegetables before beginning the curry, while the quinoa cooks.

seitan gyro bowl

SERVES 4 | SF

Gyros and I have had a longtime love affair. Some cooks love Reuben sandwiches in any form, and I feel the same about gyros. I have transformed this sandwich into a bowl, and I love every bite. If you have time, make the Quick Pickled Onions (page 114) to top this bowl.

QUINOA

1 cup quinoa, rinsed well

1 1/2 cups vegetable broth

1 garlic clove, crushed

1 teaspoon fresh or 1/2 teaspoon dried oregano

1/4 teaspoon fresh or dried rosemary

1/4 teaspoon sea salt

MARINADE

2 tablespoons olive oil

1 tablespoon fresh lemon juice

4 garlic cloves, minced

1 teaspoon fresh or dried rosemary

1 teaspoon fresh or dried oregano

Sea salt and black pepper

1 pound Slow-Simmered Seitan (page 11) or store-bought, cut into 1/2-inch strips

VEGETABLES

4 cups chopped vegetables (carrot, sweet potato, squash, green beans, etc.)

8 ounces kale, tough stems removed, chopped

1 teaspoon grapeseed oil

Sea salt and black pepper

SAUCE

1/4 cup thin-style tahini

1/4 cup unsweetened plain vegan yogurt

2 tablespoons fresh lemon juice

2 tablespoons water

1 garlic clove

Sea salt and black pepper

GARNISHES

1 medium ripe tomato, coarsely chopped

1/2 small red onion, cut into paper-thin slices

1/2 teaspoon olive oil

2 pita breads, toasted and cut into small squares

QUINOA: Heat the quinoa, broth, garlic, oregano, rosemary, and salt in a small saucepan. Cover, bring to boil over high heat, reduce to medium-low heat, cover and cook for 15 minutes. Remove from heat and set aside for 10 minutes. Fluff with fork before serving.

MARINADE: Combine the oil, lemon juice, garlic, rosemary, oregano, and salt and pepper to taste in a medium bowl. Add the seitan and mix well. Set aside for 5 minutes. Heat a large skillet over medium heat, add the seitan and cook until golden brown, about 8 minutes, stirring as needed. Cook the seitan in batches to prevent crowding. Set aside.

VEGETABLES: Prepare a steamer basket in a large pot. Steam the hard vegetables (carrot, etc.) for 7 minutes before adding the softer vegetables (green beans, etc.). Continue steaming for 4 minutes and add the kale. Steam until all the vegetables are tender, about 5 more minutes. Drizzle the vegetables with the oil and season with salt and black pepper. Keep warm.

SAUCE: Combine the tahini, yogurt, lemon juice, water, and garlic in a small blender. Blend until smooth. Taste and season with salt and pepper. Set aside.

GARNISHES: Combine the tomato, onion and oil in a small bowl. Season with salt and pepper. Set aside. Serve the vegetables in bowls topped with the quinoa. Add seitan on top of the quinoa and garnish with the salad and toasted pita chips. Drizzle with the sauce.

 QUICK TIPS: Heat the broth for the quinoa, then prepare 3 tablespoons of lemon juice. Prepare the vegetables for steaming while the seitan marinates and cooks. Make the sauce and garnish while the vegetables and seitan cook. Toast the pita just before serving.

philly cheesesteak bowl (page 58)

four | sautéed bowls

The bowls in this chapter are made with quick-cooking sautéed ingredients, giving you all the flavor and aroma you'd expect from a meal that took hours to prepare. These recipes show you how to achieve layers of great flavors in a short amount of time. Try a lighter, faster, and vegan version of brasoi, my childhood favorite, made with chickpeas and roasted potatoes tossed in a garlic-paprika sauce. It makes me hungry just thinking about it! Or how about the super-fast Roman-Style Tempeh smothered with stewed peppers and served with a kale salad? From a casual Philly Cheesesteak Bowl to a Holiday Bowl with all the trimmings, this chapter has delicious bowl meals for all occasions.

lentil picadillo bowl

SERVES 4 | GFO, SF

Picadillo is a traditional Latin American sauté consisting of meat, flavorings and tomato. The dish is often sweetened in some way, using sugar, honey or even raisins. This rendition of picadillo is the Puerto Rican version, which includes achiote seeds, olives and raisins. Nutritious lentils replace the ground meat.

LENTILS

- 5 cups water
- 1/2 cup green lentils, picked over and rinsed
- 1/2 cup brown lentils, picked over and rinsed
- 2 bay leaves

FARRO

- 3 cups vegetable broth
- 1 cup pearled farro, rinsed well
- 1 teaspoon sea salt

SPICES

- 2 teaspoons black peppercorns
- 2 teaspoons cumin seeds
- 2 teaspoons coriander seeds
- 2 teaspoons achiote (annatto) seeds
- 2 teaspoons dried oregano
- 2 teaspoons paprika

SAUTÉ

- 1 medium onion, cut into large chunks
- 1 red bell pepper, cut into large chunks
- 8 garlic cloves
- 1/2 cup cilantro
- 2 tablespoons olive oil
- 6 tablespoons tomato paste
- 1/2 cup red wine
- 8 ounces kale, tough stems removed and coarsely chopped
- 1 cup vegetable broth
- 1 cup pitted Spanish olives, sliced
- 1/2 cup raisins
- 1 1/2 teaspoons sea salt
- 1/2 cup toasted pepitas (pumpkin seeds) (optional)

GLUTEN-FREE OPTION: Substitute 30-Minute Brown Rice (page 16) or cooked white rice for the farro.

LENTILS: Combine the water, lentils and bay leaves in a medium saucepan and bring to boil. Reduce to a simmer and cook until the lentils are al dente, about 20 minutes. Drain, reserving 1/2 cup of cooking liquid and return the lentils to the pan.

FARRO: Heat the broth, farro and salt in a medium saucepan over high heat. Bring to boil, reduce to simmer and cook until tender, about 20 minutes. Drain, return to the pan and keep warm.

SPICES: Combine the peppercorn, cumin, coriander, achiote, oregano, and paprika in a spice grinder or personal blender. Process until finely ground. Add 2 tablespoons of the mixture to the lentils as they cook.

SAUTÉ: Add the onion, bell pepper, garlic and cilantro to a food processor. Process until finely ground. Heat the oil in a large pot over high heat. Stir in the vegetable mixture and cook until most of the liquid has evaporated, about 5 minutes. Add the tomato paste and cook for 30 seconds. Add the wine and cook until the wine evaporates, about 3 minutes. Add the rest of the spice mixture, kale, broth, olives, raisins and salt. Cover and cook until the kale softens, about 5 minutes. Stir in the drained lentils and reserved cooking liquid and cook, uncovered, until the flavors meld, about 5 minutes. Divide the farro among 4 bowls, top with the lentil sauté. and garnish with pepitas, if using.

QUICK TIPS: Begin by heating the broth for the farro and the water for the lentils. Make the spice mixture while the lentils are cooking.

SUBSTITUTIONS: Use all of one type of lentil (brown or green). Substitute 1/2 teaspoon ground turmeric and 1/2 teaspoon tamarind concentrate for the achiote seeds. Add the tamarind directly to the stew along with the wine. Substitute pearled barley, soaked overnight, for the farro,

kidney bean cottage pie bowl

SERVES 4 | GFO, SF

Cottage pie is believed to be the ancestor of shepherd's pie, a meat and vegetable casserole covered with mashed potatoes. This take on the classic dish is a hearty, robust stew of kidney beans and vegetables with a mashed potato topping.

POTATOES

2 pounds Yukon Gold potatoes, peeled and cut
   into 1/2-inch dice
4 garlic cloves, crushed
1 teaspoon sea salt
1 sprig fresh rosemary
1/4 to 1/2 cup unsweetened plain nondairy milk
2 tablespoons olive oil
Black pepper, to taste

BEANS AND VEGETABLES

2 tablespoons olive oil
1 medium onion, finely chopped
8 ounces turnips, cut into 1/2-inch dice
2 medium carrots, cut into 1/2-inch dice
4 garlic cloves, minced
10 sprigs fresh thyme
1 teaspoon sea salt
1/4 cup whole-wheat pastry flour or all-purpose
   flour
2 tablespoons tomato paste
2/3 cup red wine
2 cups cooked cannellini beans
2 cups cooked kidney beans
2 cups vegetable broth
4 cups fresh baby spinach
Black pepper
1 cup green peas, thawed if frozen

GLUTEN-FREE OPTION: Omit the flour. Mix 1/2 cup of the broth with 1 1/2 tablespoons organic cornstarch or arrowroot starch. Add the slurry to the sauté after the spinach wilts and simmer just to thicken.

POTATOES: Combine the potatoes, garlic, salt, and rosemary in a medium saucepan. Add just enough water to cover, bring to a boil over high heat, covered, reduce to simmer over medium and cook until knife-tender, about 10 minutes. Drain, discard the rosemary stem, mash with a potato masher, and add 1/4 cup of milk, oil and pepper. Stir with a sturdy wooden spoon, adding more milk, if needed, and keep warm. If you have extra time, transfer the potatoes to a baking sheet in 1/4 cup portions and bake in a preheated 450°F oven until crisp on top, about 15 minutes.

BEANS AND VEGETABLES: Heat the oil in a large skillet over medium heat. Add the onion, cover and cook until softened, about 5 minutes, stirring occasionally. Add the turnips, carrot, garlic, thyme, and salt. Cook covered, stirring occasionally, until golden, about 5 more minutes. Stir in the flour and mix until well combined. Stir in the tomato paste and cook 1 minute. Stir in the wine and cook until evaporated, about 2 minutes.

Add the beans and broth to the skillet. Cook until the sauce is reduced by one quarter, about 3 minutes. Taste and adjust seasoning with salt and pepper. Add the spinach and cook until wilted, about 2 minutes. Remove from heat and stir in the peas. Cover and keep warm until serving. To serve, spoon the beans and vegetables into bowls and top with the mashed potatoes.

QUICK TIPS: Heat the water for the potatoes while you peel and chop the potatoes. Prepare the turnips and carrots while the onion cooks. Preheat the oven to 450°F if opting to bake the potatoes. Use an ice cream scoop to portion the potatoes before baking.

tempeh paprikás

SERVES 4 | GFO, SFO

Paprikás is a cousin to goulash, the famous Hungarian stew. This variation adds sour cream to the stew, thickening it and adding some tang. In this recipe I serve the paprikás with a quick cabbage salad and homemade dumplings.

SALAD

- 4 cups finely sliced green cabbage
- 1/2 teaspoon sea salt
- 1 medium carrot, shredded
- 2 tablespoons white wine vinegar
- 2 tablespoons water
- Pinch paprika and black pepper

TEMPEH

- 1 teaspoon toasted sesame oil
- 8 ounces tempeh, cut into 1/4-inch dice
- 1 tablespoon grapeseed oil
- 1 large onion, finely chopped
- 4 garlic cloves, minced
- 1/4 cup whole wheat pastry or all-purpose flour
- 1 large bell pepper, cut into 1/2-inch dice
- 1 large tomato, cut into 1/2-inch dice
- 1 tablespoon Hungarian paprika
- 2 cups vegetable broth
- 1 teaspoon sea salt
- 1 cup Cashew Sour Cream Sauce (page 10) or storebought

NOKEDLI

- 1 cup unsweetened plain nondairy milk
- 4 tablespoons flaxseed meal or ground flaxseeds
- 1 1/2 teaspoons sea salt
- Pinch ground turmeric
- 2 cups whole-wheat pastry or all-purpose flour

GLUTEN-FREE OPTION: Omit the flour. Mix 1/2 cup of the broth with 1 tablespoon organic cornstarch or arrowroot. Add the slurry to the paprikás with the cashew sauce and simmer just to thicken. Omit the nokedli and serve with cooked gluten-free pasta or rice.

SOY-FREE OPTION: Substitute 12 ounces of diced seitan for the tempeh.

SALAD: Combine the cabbage and salt in a medium bowl. Massage the cabbage to tenderize it and set aside for 15 minutes. Drain the cabbage and add the carrot, vinegar, water and paprika. Season with black pepper.

TEMPEH: Heat the sesame oil in a large skillet over medium heat. Add the tempeh and cook, stirring often, until golden. Transfer the tempeh to a medium bowl and set aside. Add the grapeseed oil to the skillet. Add the onion and garlic, cover and cook until softened, about 3 minutes. Add the flour, stir and cook until the flour smells nutty, about 3 minutes. Add the bell pepper and tomato, cover and cook until softened, about 2 minutes. Stir in the tempeh, paprika, broth and salt. Bring to boil, reduce to simmer. Cook until the vegetables are tender, about 3 minutes. Stir in the sour cream and cook for about 2 minutes. Keep warm.

NOKEDLI: Bring a medium saucepan of water to boil. Combine the milk, flax meal, salt and turmeric, stirring well. Set aside for 5 minutes to thicken. Stir in the flour and mix well. Transfer the dough to a medium cutting board, flattening it to about 1 x 3 inches wide. Perch the board on the edge of the pan of water and, using a paring knife, cut off long slices of dough, about 1/4-inch wide, pushing them off the board and into the boiling water. Repeat until all the dough is used, stirring the pan of water with the knife occasionally. Cook the nokedli for a few minutes after they have risen to the top of the water. Drain and serve with the paprikás and salad.

QUICK TIPS: Heat the water for the nokedli right away. Prepare the cabbage for the salad first. Chop the tempeh, onion and garlic before cooking the tempeh. Chop the bell pepper and tomato while the tempeh cooks.

sin carne guisada bowl

SERVES 4 TO 6 | GFO, SFO

Carne guisada is a Mexican beef stew that is often served with corn tortillas. I include jackfruit in this recipe for much-needed texture. Young green jackfruit, most commonly found canned in brine, is inherently flavorless, but it effectively soaks up whatever it is cooked in. Since the jackfruit is strictly for the texture, the flavor of this dish comes from the sofrito, a Latin American sauce of braised onions, bell peppers and tomatoes. Do not use ripe, or sweet, jackfruit in this recipe. Serve with corn tortillas if desired.

RICE

- 1 1/2 cups water
- 1/2 teaspoon sea salt
- 1 cup long-grain white rice
- 1 cup peas, thawed if frozen

SOFRITO

- 4 garlic cloves
- 2 small Roma tomatoes, coarsely chopped
- 1 medium onion, coarsely chopped
- 1 medium green bell pepper, coarsely chopped
- 1 small jalapeño chile, coarsely chopped
- 2 tablespoons minced soft sun-dried tomatoes

STEW

- 2 tablespoons grapeseed oil
- 1 (20-ounce) can green jackfruit, in brine or water, rinsed well, lightly squeezed, coarsely chopped
- 1 teaspoon ground cumin
- 1 teaspoon dried oregano
- 1 teaspoon natural sugar
- 1 teaspoon sea salt
- 1/3 cup whole-wheat or all-purpose flour
- 2 tablespoons tomato paste
- 3 cups vegetable broth
- 1 tablespoon reduced-sodium tamari
- 2 cups cooked black beans
- 1 teaspoon paprika

VEGETABLES

- 3 cups coarsely chopped cauliflower florets
- Sea salt and black pepper

SOY-FREE OPTION: Substitute coconut aminos and 1/8 teaspoon sea salt for the tamari.

RICE: Heat the water and salt in a small saucepan over high heat. Rinse the rice in two changes of fresh water and add to the pan. When the water is bubbling on the sides of the pan, cover the pan, reduce the heat to low and cook for 15 minutes. Remove from the heat and set aside for 10 minutes to steam. Add the peas and fluff with a fork. Keep warm.

SOFRITO: Add the garlic to a food processor and process until minced. Add the tomato, onion, bell pepper, jalapeño and sun-dried tomato. Process until finely ground. Set aside.

STEW: Heat the oil in a large skillet over medium-high heat. Add the reserved sofrito, jackfruit, cumin, oregano, sugar and salt. Cook, stirring occasionally, until the skillet is dry, about 10 minutes. Add the flour, stirring well, and cook for 3 minutes. Add the tomato paste and cook for 1 minute. Add the broth, tamari, beans and paprika. Stir well and bring to boil. Reduce heat to medium and simmer until the jackfruit is tender, breaking up the jackfruit with a spatula as it cooks, about 10 minutes.

VEGETABLES: Steam the cauliflower in a large pot with a steamer basket until tender, about 8 minutes. Season with salt and black pepper and keep warm. Sever the rice in large shallow bowls, topped with the stew and alongside the steamed cauliflower.

QUICK TIPS: Chop the tomato, onion and peppers into large pieces, as the food processor will be doing most of the work. Preheat the skillet while you process the sofrito.

GLUTEN-FREE OPTION: Omit the flour. Mix 1/2 cup of the broth with 2 tablespoons cornstarch; add to the stew at the end of the cooking; simmer to thicken.

korean bulgogi with black bean ssamjang

SERVES 4 | GF

Bulgogi is Korean barbecue that is served in lettuce leaves. The marinade is sweet and lightly salty and utterly delicious. Don't let the specialty ingredients throw you, since they have substitutes, if preferred. Doenjang is Korea's fermented soybean paste, akin to miso, but fermented longer with much less sweetness. Ssamjang is a spicy paste that is usually added to foods that are eaten wrapped in lettuce leaves. It is often combined with other ingredients such as tofu or, as in this case, beans, to enhance its flavor, nutrition, and texture.

MARINADE

- 1/4 cup vegetable broth
- 1/4 cup reduced-sodium tamari
- 1 tablespoon toasted sesame oil
- 3 tablespoons natural sugar
- 1 medium Asian pear, peeled and finely grated
- 1/2 small onion, cut into 1/8-inch slices
- 4 garlic cloves, minced
- 2 scallions, minced
- 1 pound portobello mushrooms, stemmed and gills scraped, cut into 1/2-inch thick slices
- 1 tablespoon toasted sesame seeds

SSAMJANG

- 2 tablespoons fermented bean paste (doenjang)
- 2 teaspoons Korean red pepper paste (gochujang)
- 1 teaspoon toasted sesame oil
- 1 teaspoon natural sugar
- 1 cup cooked black beans
- 1 scallion, minced
- 2 teaspoons toasted sesame seeds
- Sea salt and black pepper

SALAD

- 1 cucumber, peeled, thinly sliced, and squeezed
- 2 scallions, minced
- 1 tablespoon rice vinegar
- 1 teaspoon toasted sesame oil
- 1 teaspoon reduced-sodium tamari
- Sea salt and black pepper

NOODLES

- 4 ounces thin rice noodles (mai fun)
- Romaine or butter lettuce leaves, to serve

MARINADE: Combine the broth, tamari, oil, sugar, pear, onion, garlic, and scallions in a large bowl. Mix well and add the mushrooms. Toss well to coat and set aside to marinade while the skillet preheats, about 5 minutes. Preheat a large skillet over medium-high heat. Drain the mushrooms and add to the skillet. Cook until golden brown, about 5 minutes, stirring occasionally to help the mushrooms sear. Add the remaining marinade to the skillet and cook until sauce evaporates and the mushrooms are tender, about 3 minutes. Take care not to burn the sauce. Set aside and garnish with the sesame seeds.

SSAMJANG: Combine the bean paste, red pepper paste, oil and sugar in a medium bowl. Mix well and fold in the black beans, scallions and sesame seeds. Taste and adjust seasoning with salt and pepper. Set aside.

SALAD: Combine the cucumber, scallions, vinegar, oil and tamari in a small bowl. Mix well, season with salt and pepper and set aside.

NOODLES: Bring a medium pot of water to boil. Add the noodles and cook, stirring, until al dente, about 2 minutes. Drain. Rinse under cool water, drain well and coarsely chop.

ASSEMBLY: Serve the bulgogi in wide shallow bowls. Place the mushrooms, noodles, salad, and ssamjang side by side in the bowl. To eat, layer the ingredients as desired in lettuce leaves and devour.

GLUTEN-FREE CAUTION: Make sure your fermented bean paste is gluten-free, as there are some brands that use wheat in the fermentation.

SUBSTITUTION: Substitute Bosc pear or another firm pear for the Asian pear (also known as apple pear). Substitute dark miso (not white) for the doenjang. Substitute sambal oelek or sriracha for the gochujang. Substitute cremini mushrooms for the portobellos.

QUICK TIPS: Begin by heating the water for the noodles; keep the pot covered until needed. Allow the mushrooms to marinate while you prepare the ssamjang. Heat the skillet while you prepare the salad. Use a vegetable peeler to cut the cucumber into thin slices, rotating the cucumber as you cut. Stop peeling when you reach the seeds of the cucumber. Squeeze the slices of cucumber using your hands.

seitan ossobuco bowl

SERVES 4 | SF

Ossobuco is a Milanese braise of meat and vegetables in a wine broth. Traditionally the dish is braised for many hours to tenderize the meat and is then served with gremolata, a lemon-garlic-parsley mince. In my version, seitan is braised in the delicious reduction and is then served over polenta with the gremolata. Really decadent and satisfying.

SAUCE

- 1 teaspoon olive oil
- 1 medium onion, finely chopped
- 1 medium carrot, cut into half moons
- 1 teaspoon fresh or dried rosemary
- 1 teaspoon fresh or dried thyme
- 3 tablespoons tomato paste
- 3/4 cup white wine, dry sherry or dry vermouth
- 3 cups vegetable broth
- 3 cups chopped zucchini, cut into 1/2-inch dice (about 1 medium)
- Sea salt and black pepper

POLENTA

- 3 cups vegetable broth
- 1/2 teaspoon sea salt
- 1 1/4 cups polenta
- 1 1/2 cups unsweetened plain nondairy milk, divided

SEITAN

- 1 pound Slow-Simmered Seitan (page 11) or store-bought seitan, cut into 1/2-inch thick slices
- 3 tablespoons whole-wheat pastry flour or all-purpose flour
- Sea salt and black pepper
- 2 tablespoons olive oil, divided

GREMOLATA

- 1/2 cup very finely minced parsley
- 2 garlic cloves, very finely minced
- Zest of 2 lemons, finely minced

SAUCE: Heat the oil in a large pot over medium heat. Add the onion, carrot, rosemary and thyme, cover and cook until softened, about 5 minutes, stirring occasionally. Add the tomato paste, stir and cook until golden, about 1 minute. Stir in the wine and cook until the wine evaporates. Stir in the broth and cook over medium-high heat until the sauce reduces by almost half, about 12 minutes. Add the zucchini and cook until tender, about 4 minutes. Season to taste with salt and pepper.

POLENTA: Heat the broth and salt in a medium saucepan, covered, over high heat until boiling. Stir in the polenta with a whisk and simmer over medium heat until thickened, 2 to 5 minutes. Stir in 1 cup of milk and simmer over low heat until the polenta is tender, 10 to 15 minutes, partly covered. Stir in the remaining 1/2 cup of milk right before serving if the polenta is too thick. Taste and adjust seasoning with salt and pepper.

SEITAN: Combine the seitan and flour in a medium bowl. Add salt and pepper to taste. Heat 1 tablespoon of oil in a large skillet over medium heat. Cook half the seitan until golden brown, about 2 minutes per side. Transfer the seitan to the simmering sauce. Repeat with the remaining oil and seitan.

GREMOLATA: Combine the parsley, garlic and zest in a small bowl. Alternatively, mince the ingredients in a food processor. Serve the polenta in bowls topped with the seitan and sauce, garnished with the gremolata.

QUICK TIPS: Chop the onion and begin cooking it while you chop the carrot. Heat the broth for the polenta and measure out the polenta while the onion and carrot are sautéing. Chop the zucchini while the seitan is browning. Make the gremolata while the zucchini is cooking.

asopao de non pollo bowl

SERVES 4 | GF, SFO

This is a Puerto Rican dish that is a cross between a soup, a stew, paella and risotto; "Asopao" means "soupy." I make this dish using tempeh, but black beans are a welcome substitution. The spice mixture is my take on Sazón and adobo seasonings, the popular seasoning mixes of Latin American cuisine.

RICE

- 5 cups vegetable broth
- 1 teaspoon sea salt
- 1 teaspoon grapeseed oil
- 1 cup long-grain brown rice

SPICES

- 2 teaspoons black peppercorns
- 2 teaspoons cumin seeds
- 2 teaspoons coriander seeds
- 2 teaspoons achiote (annatto) seeds
- 2 teaspoons dried oregano
- 3 teaspoons smoked paprika
- 6 garlic cloves, minced
- 1 tablespoon fresh lime juice
- 8 ounces tempeh, cut into 1-inch cubes
- 1 tablespoon grapeseed oil

VEGETABLES

- 1 medium onion, coarsely chopped
- 1 medium green bell pepper, coarsely chopped
- 6 tablespoons tomato paste
- 8 ounces collard greens, tough stems removed, cut into 1/4-inch slices
- 1 cup green peas, partially thawed if frozen
- 1 ripe Hass avocado, pitted, peeled and coarsely chopped

SOY-FREE OPTION: Substitute 2 cups cooked black beans for the tempeh.

RICE: Heat the vegetable broth and salt in a large pot, covered, over high heat. Heat the oil in a large skillet over medium heat and add the rice. Cook, stirring, until lightly browned, about 3 minutes. Add the rice to the broth. Bring to boil and reduce to simmer over medium heat. Cook until tender, about 25 minutes, or until needed.

SPICES: Heat a small skillet over medium heat. Add the peppercorns, cumin, coriander, and achiote seeds. Cook, stirring, until fragrant, about 2 minutes. Transfer the seeds to a spice grinder or small blender. Add the oregano and paprika. Process until finely ground and transfer to a medium bowl. Add the garlic and lime juice and mix well. Add the tempeh and rub the marinade into the tempeh. Heat the oil in the large skillet over medium heat. Add the tempeh and cook until golden, about 3 minutes, stirring occasionally. Add the tempeh to the broth mixture.

VEGETABLES: Add the onion and pepper to a food processor and pulse until finely ground. Add the mixture to the now empty large skillet and cook until dry, about 4 minutes. Stir in the tomato paste and cook until slightly darkened, about 3 minutes. Add the mixture to the broth along with the collard greens. Continue to cook until the rice is tender. Add the peas and remove from the heat. Taste and adjust the seasonings with salt and black pepper, if needed. Serve in bowls topped with the chopped avocado.

QUICK TIPS: Measure and add the peppercorns and seeds right into the small skillet as it is heating. Cut the tempeh while the seeds are toasting. Cut near the stove to keep an eye on the skillet. Chop the onion and bell pepper into large chunks since the food processor will do most of the work. Clean and chop the collards while the vegetables are cooking.

holiday bowl

SERVES 4 | GFO, SF

This bowl is truly a complete holiday meal, including green beans, gravy, dressing, cauli-potato mash, and even cranberries. Whenever the mood strikes and you are longing for a bit of the season, whip up this bowl and relish some familiar favorite flavors.

BROTH

- 1 1/2 cups vegetable broth
- 1 teaspoon dried sage
- 1/2 teaspoon fennel seeds
- 1/4 teaspoon red pepper flakes

STUFFING

- 1 pound oyster mushrooms, trimmed and torn into bite-size pieces
- 3 tablespoons olive oil, divided
- Sea salt and black pepper
- 4 slices bread (5 to 6 ounces), cut into 1/2-inch dice
- 1/4 cup chopped raw pecans
- 1 large onion, finely chopped
- 2 garlic cloves, minced

POTATOES

- 1 pound Yukon Gold potatoes, peeled and cut into 1-inch cubes
- 1 pound cauliflower florets
- 1 garlic clove, crushed
- 1 teaspoon sea salt
- 1 tablespoon unsweetened, plain nondairy milk

BEANS

- 2 tablespoons olive oil
- 8 ounces green beans, trimmed and cut diagonally into thin strips
- 1/2 cup dried cranberries
- Sea salt and black pepper

GRAVY

- 2 large carrots, shredded
- 2 garlic cloves, coarsely chopped
- 2 tablespoons whole wheat pastry or all-purpose flour
- 1 cup vegetable broth
- Sea salt and black pepper

BROTH: Combine the broth, sage, fennel, and red pepper flakes in a small saucepan over high heat. Bring to boil and reduce to a simmer over low heat until needed.

STUFFING: Preheat the oven to 450°F. Toss the mushrooms with 1 teaspoon olive oil, season with salt and black pepper and transfer to a baking sheet. Bake until tender, about 10 minutes, and transfer to a large bowl. Transfer the bread cubes to a separate baking sheet and bake until crisp, about 7 minutes. Add the pecans to the bread and bake an additional 3 minutes. Transfer to the large bowl with the mushrooms.

Heat 1 tablespoon oil in a large skillet over medium-high heat. Add the onion, cover and cook until softened, about 5 minutes, stirring occasionally. Add the garlic and cook for 1 minute. Transfer to the bowl with the mushrooms. Add just enough of the broth mixture to moisten the bread without making it soggy. Season with salt and pepper. Transfer the stuffing to a baking sheet, drizzle with the remaining 1 1/2 tablespoons olive oil, and bake until crunchy on top, about 10 minutes.

POTATOES: Combine the potatoes, cauliflower, garlic, salt, and enough water to cover in a medium saucepan over high heat. Bring to boil and reduce to simmer. Cook until tender, about 15 minutes. Drain and mash, adding the milk, if needed. Season with salt and pepper and set aside but keep warm.

BEANS: Heat the oil in a large skillet over medium-high heat. Add the green beans and cook until al dente, about 5 minutes. Add the cranberries and cook until tender, about 2 minutes. Season with salt and pepper. Remove and set aside.

GRAVY: Add the carrots and garlic to the now-empty skillet and cook until tender, about 3 minutes. Add the flour and cook for 1 minute, stirring well. Transfer the carrot mixture to a blender and add the broth. Season with salt and pepper and blend until smooth. Return to the skillet and cook to thicken, about 1 minute. To serve, spoon the mashed potatoes in shallow bowls, top with the stuffing, gravy, and green beans.

GLUTEN-FREE OPTION: Use gluten-free bread for the stuffing. Omit the flour when making the gravy. Add 1 tablespoon organic cornstarch or arrowroot starch to the broth and mix well. Add the slurry to the blender with the carrots and blend well. Return the gravy to the skillet to heat and thicken, if needed.

SUBSTITUTION: Substitute 1 link of vegan sausage, cut into 1/4-inch dice, for the mushrooms. Sauté the sausage with the onion until golden brown. Omit the fennel seeds from the broth.

QUICK TIPS: First, preheat the oven to 450°F, then prepare the bread for toasting and cook the potatoes and cauliflower.

roman-style tempeh bowl
with kale and apple salad

SERVES 4 | GF, SFO

Roman-style dishes, also known as Saltimbocca ala Romana, are quickly made Italian meals of thinly sliced protein and sage cooked in a light wine sauce. Thin sliced tempeh fits the bill perfectly here, and I've added sweet potatoes and red bell peppers to the sauté. The massaged kale salad is a refreshing change from pasta or a heavier starch, but you can certainly serve this bowl over cooked pasta.

TEMPEH

2 tablespoons arrowroot or organic cornstarch

Sea salt and black pepper

8 ounces tempeh, cut in half

1 tablespoon olive oil

SAUTÉ

1 tablespoon olive oil

1 teaspoon toasted sesame oil

2 medium red bell peppers, cut into 1/4-inch slices

1 medium onion, cut into 1/4-inch slices

4 garlic cloves, minced

1 teaspoon dried sage

1/2 teaspoon red pepper flakes

Sea salt and black pepper

1 cup dry sherry or dry white wine

2 medium ripe tomatoes, chopped

1 1/2 cups vegetable broth

2 sweet potatoes, peeled, cut into 1/2-inch dice

KALE

3 tablespoons fresh lemon juice

1 tablespoon olive oil

1/2 teaspoon sea salt

Black pepper, to taste

8 ounces kale, stemmed, cut into 1/4-inch slices

1 medium apple, any variety, cut into julienne slices

SOY-FREE OPTION: Substitute 3 cups cooked large lima beans for the tempeh. Mix 1/4 cup of broth with 2 tablespoons cornstarch and set aside. Omit the tempeh ingredients and instructions. Add the beans to the sauté at the time you would add the tempeh. Stir in the cornstarch slurry after the potatoes are tender and simmer to thicken.

TEMPEH: Combine the starch with salt and pepper, to taste, in a shallow pan. Cut each tempeh half into two triangles. Cut each triangle in half through the middle, creating thin tempeh triangles. Dredge the tempeh in the seasoned cornstarch. Heat the oil in a large pot over medium-high heat. Pan-fry the tempeh until golden brown, 2 minutes per side. Transfer to a plate and set aside.

SAUTÉ: Heat the oils in the large pot. Add the bell peppers, onions, garlic, sage, and red pepper flakes. Cover and cook until the vegetables soften, about 5 minutes, stirring occasionally. Season with salt and pepper. Add the sherry and tomatoes. Return the tempeh to the pot. Cook until the sherry evaporates almost completely. Add the broth and potato, bring to a boil and reduce to a strong simmer over medium heat. Cover and cook until the vegetables are tender and the flavors have melded, 5 to 7 minutes. Uncover and continue to cook until the sauce thickens. Taste and adjust seasoning.

KALE: Combine the lemon juice, olive oil, salt, and pepper in a large bowl. Add the kale and, using both your hands, massage the marinade into the kale. Use a firm hand in order to break down the cell walls of the tough kale leaves; this should take about 1 minute. Add the apple slices and mix to combine. Taste and adjust the seasoning, if needed. Serve the sauté in bowls with the kale.

QUICK TIPS: Prepare the bell peppers, onion, and garlic before cooking the tempeh. Make the kale salad while the sauté cooks.

braised greek kabocha squash bowl

SERVES 4 | GF, SF

The Greek influence is evident in this dish with the abundance of garlic, olive oil, oregano, lemon, and dill. Kabocha is perfect for braising because its texture is starchy and dry when cooked without too much liquid. In this recipe, it is first roasted to impart extra flavor and to speed its cooking time.

SQUASH

1/2 medium kabocha squash (about 1 pound), seeded and cut into 3/4-inch cubes
1 tablespoon olive oil
Sea salt and black pepper, to taste

QUINOA

4 cups vegetable broth
1 cup quinoa, rinsed

SEASONING

1 small onion, coarsely chopped
4 scallions, coarsely chopped
4 garlic cloves
2 tablespoons olive oil
2 teaspoons dried oregano
1/2 cup dill weed
Zest of 1 lemon
1/2 teaspoon sea salt

BRAISE

2 large plum tomatoes, coarsely chopped
1/4 to 1/2 teaspoon red pepper flakes
8 ounces tatzoi or fresh mature spinach

SQUASH: Preheat the oven to 450°F. Combine the squash, olive oil, salt and pepper on a baking sheet. Bake until golden, about 15 minutes, stirring midway through baking. Set aside.

QUINOA: Combine the broth and quinoa in a medium saucepan over high heat. Bring to boil, then reduce to simmer over medium-low heat. Cook until needed, about 10 minutes.

SEASONING: Add the onion, scallions and garlic to a food processor. Process until finely ground. Add the oil, oregano, dill, zest and salt. Process to combine.

BRAISE: Heat a large pot over medium-high heat. Add the onion mixture and cook until golden, about 4 minutes, stirring often. Add the tomatoes and red pepper flakes and cook until the tomatoes are broken down, about 3 more minutes. Add the quinoa mixture, reduce to medium heat and bring to a strong simmer. Cook until tender. Add the roasted squash when it is ready. Add the tatzoi when the quinoa and squash are tender and the sauce has reduced to about 1/2 cup. Cook until tender, about 2 minutes. Serve.

 QUICK TIPS: Begin by preheating the oven to 450°F and heating the broth for the quinoa. Keep covered until you add the quinoa. Cut the squash while the broth is heating up. Prepare the seasoning while the large pot preheats.

PREPARING THE SQUASH: Kabocha squash does not need to be peeled, as its skin is edible. Some kabocha have knobby growths that need to be trimmed, if you opt not to peel the squash. Scrub the squash well and cut in half. Use an ice cream scoop to easily remove the seeds. Place the squash cut side down and slice as needed. Many grocers will cut the squash in half for you, if you ask.

enchilada bowl with pumpkin cream sauce

SERVES 4 | GFO, SF

These enchiladas are filled with black beans, root vegetables and spinach. They are served over couscous and topped with a creamy pumpkin sauce. Enchiladas typically bring to mind hours in the kitchen, but this recipe is quickly cooked and assembled. For gluten-free, substitute 2 cups cooked rice for the couscous.

COUSCOUS

- 2 teaspoons grapeseed oil
- 1/2 medium onion, finely chopped
- 2 garlic cloves, minced
- 1 1/4 cups plus 2 tablespoons vegetable broth
- 1/2 teaspoon sea salt
- 1 cup instant whole-wheat couscous

FILLING

- 2 teaspoons grapeseed oil
- 1/2 medium onion, finely chopped
- 1 large carrot, cut into 1/4-inch dice
- 4 ounces turnip, cut into 1/4-inch dice
- 2 garlic cloves, minced
- 1/4 cup vegetable broth, divided
- 2 cups cooked black beans
- 2 teaspoon Chipotle Purée (page 14)
- 4 cups fresh baby spinach
- Sea salt and black pepper
- 1 cup corn kernels, thawed and drained if frozen
- 8 (5-inch) corn tortillas

SAUCE

- 2 teaspoons grapeseed oil
- 3 scallions, finely chopped
- 2 garlic cloves, minced
- 3/4 teaspoons ground cumin
- 1/2 to 3/4 cup coconut milk
- 1 (15-ounce) can solid-pack pumpkin
- 1 tablespoon fresh lime juice
- 1/2 to 1 teaspoon natural sugar
- Sea salt and black pepper
- 1/2 cup toasted pistachios, chopped

COUSCOUS: Heat the oil in a small saucepan over medium-high heat. Add the onion, cover and cook until softened, about 5 minutes, stirring occasionally. Add the garlic and cook until fragrant, 30 seconds. Add 2 tablespoons of the broth, cover and cook until the onion is tender. Add the remaining 1 1/4 cups broth and salt, cover, and bring to a boil. Transfer the broth to a large bowl and add the couscous. Cover the bowl and set aside until all the broth is absorbed, about 10 minutes.

FILLING: Heat the oil in a medium saucepan over medium-high heat. Add the onion, cover and cook until softened, about 5 minutes, stirring occasionally. Add the carrot, turnip, garlic and 2 tablespoons broth. Cover and cook until almost tender, about 4 minutes. Add the beans, chipotle and remaining 2 tablespoons broth. Cover and cook until the turnip is tender, about 4 more minutes. Add the spinach and cook to wilt, about 2 minutes. Season with salt and pepper. Heat a large skillet over medium heat. Add the corn and cook, stirring occasionally, until golden, about 7 minutes. Transfer the corn to the filling with the black beans. Toast the corn tortillas individually in the skillet until pliable, about 30 seconds per side. Transfer the tortillas to a folded kitchen towel to keep warm.

SAUCE: Heat the oil in the now empty small saucepan over medium-high heat. Add the scallions, garlic, and cumin. Cook until fragrant, about 1 minute. Add the coconut milk and bring to boil. Stir in the pumpkin, lime, and sugar. Mix well, return to a boil, then reduce to simmer. Season with salt and pepper and cook for 4 minutes. Fluff the couscous with a fork and divide among 4 shallow bowls. Fill a tortilla with about 2 tablespoons of filling, roll up and place on the couscous. Repeat with another tortilla and ladle on about 1/4 cup of sauce. Repeat with the remaining tortillas. Serve garnished with pistachios.

 QUICK TIPS: Prepare the couscous and the filling at the same time. Chop the carrot and turnip while the onion cooks. Roast the corn after the chopping is done and add it to the filling when it is ready. Begin heating the tortillas when the corn is done cooking; they will keep warm in the towel for about 10 minutes.

irish stew bowl

SERVES 4 TO 6 | SF

A robust Irish stew brings to mind cooking in a cauldron over an open fire. The potato is a modern addition to this ancient recipe of vegetables and meat, not having been introduced to Ireland until the 16th century. My recipe utilizes farro and a variety of root vegetables and legumes.

MUSHROOMS
1 cup vegetable broth
1/2 ounce dried porcini mushrooms
8 ounces shell pasta

FARRO
4 cups vegetable broth
1/2 cup pearled farro, rinsed well
4 garlic cloves, crushed
2 bay leaves
1/2 teaspoon sea salt

STEW
2 tablespoons olive oil
1 large onion, finely chopped
1/2 medium cauliflower, cut into medium florets
1/2 medium celeriac, peeled, cut into 1/2-inch dice
1 teaspoon fennel seeds
1 teaspoon sea salt
1 (2-inch) sprig fresh rosemary
1/4 cup whole-wheat pastry flour or all-purpose flour
1/2 cup dry white wine or dry vermouth
2 cups cooked cannellini beans
4 ounces green beans, trimmed and chopped
2 teaspoons stone-ground mustard
2 teaspoons drained horseradish
1/4 cup chopped parsley
Black pepper

SUBSTITUTION: Substitute 1 medium parsnip, chopped, and 2 celery ribs, minced, for the celeriac. Substitute pearled barley, soaked overnight, for the farro.

CELERY ROOT: To peel, cut off the top of the root and place cut-side down on work surface. Using a chef knife cut away the tough outer skin. Cut into 1-inch slices and slice as needed. You must add the celeriac to boiling water to prevent it from turning bitter.

MUSHROOMS: Heat the broth in a medium saucepan over high heat. Bring to boil, add the porcini, cover, reduce to simmer, and cook for 3 minutes. Transfer the mushrooms and broth to a small bowl and set aside for 10 minutes to soften. Drain the porcini, reserving the broth, and rinse the mushrooms in a strainer. Chop the mushrooms and set aside. Strain the broth using a coffee filter or reusable tea bag and set aside. In the same medium saucepan, heat salted water to boil. Add the pasta and cook until al dente. Drain and set aside.

FARRO: Combine the broth, farro, garlic, bay leaves and salt in a medium saucepan over high heat. Cover, bring to boil and reduce to simmer. Cook until tender, 15 to 20 minutes. Remove from heat and set aside.

STEW: Heat the oil in a large pot over medium-high heat. Add the onion, cauliflower, celeriac, fennel, salt and rosemary. Cover and cook until the vegetables are golden brown, about 10 minutes, stirring occasionally. Add a few tablespoons of water if the vegetables are sticking. Add the flour to the large pot and stir well to combine. Add the wine and stir. Cook until the wine evaporates, about 2 minutes. Add the reserved porcinis and the porcini liquid, the reserved cooked farro mixture, and the cannellini and the green beans. Cook until the green beans and celeriac are tender, 5 to 8 minutes. Remove and discard the rosemary sprig and bay leaves. Stir in the mustard, horseradish and parsley. Taste and adjust seasoning with salt and pepper. Serve the pasta covered with the stew in deep bowls.

 QUICK TIPS: Begin by heating the broth for the mushrooms and farro. Add the onions to the large pot to cook first, then add the other vegetables as they are chopped. Heat the water for the pasta as soon as the mushrooms are put in the small bowl to rehydrate.

philly cheesesteak bowl

SERVES 4 | GFO, SFO

This may be the most decadent bowl in the book because it is served over tater tots. However, the bowl is equally delicious served over home fries, French fries or even baked potatoes. To make it into a sandwich, just add the filling to a soft hoagie roll. Regardless of how you serve it, this is delicious, nostalgic comforting food. If you don't have black cardamom, substitute 1/2 teaspoon liquid smoke. If you don't have tamari or tamarind, substitute 2 tablespoons vegan Worcestershire sauce. (See photo on page 38.)

1 pound frozen tater tots

CHEESE SAUCE
2/3 cup grated Yukon Gold or other waxy potato
1/2 cup raw cashew pieces
1/2 cup unsweetened plain nondairy milk
1 tablespoon jarred roasted red peppers, rinsed
1 teaspoon apple cider vinegar
1 teaspoon white miso
1 teaspoon paprika
1/4 teaspoon sea salt

AU JUS
3/4 cup vegetable broth
1 tablespoon reduced-sodium tamari
1 teaspoon tamarind concentrate
2 black cardamom pods, crushed
1/4 teaspoon fresh or dried thyme
1/4 teaspoon fresh or dried oregano

SAUTÉ
2 tablespoons olive oil, divided
1 large onion, cut into 1/8-inch slices
1/2 teaspoon sea salt
1 large bell pepper, cut into 1/4-inch slices
1 pound Slow-Simmered Seitan (page 11) or store-bought seitan, cut into 1/4-inch slices, on the bias
4 cups fresh baby spinach

GLUTEN-FREE OPTION: Substitute 1 pound of portobello mushrooms, cut into 1/2-inch slices, for the seitan.

SOY-FREE OPTION: Substitute coconut aminos and a few pinches of sea salt for the tamari. Substitute chickpea miso for the white miso.

Preheat the oven to 450°F. Spread the tater tots in a single layer on a metal baking sheet and bake until crisp, 15 to 20 minutes. (You can put them in the oven before the oven is completely preheated.) Turn the tots halfway through cooking. Remove from oven and set aside but keep warm.

CHEESE SAUCE: Combine the potato and cashews with enough water to cover in a small saucepan. Bring to boil and cook until the potato is tender, 8 to 10 minutes. Drain and rinse. Transfer to a blender and add the milk, red pepper, vinegar, miso, paprika and salt. Blend until smooth. Transfer back to the small saucepan and cook over medium heat until thickened, stirring often, about 3 minutes.

AU JUS: Combine the broth, tamari, tamarind, cardamom, thyme and oregano in a small saucepan and bring to boil, then reduce to simmer until needed, about 15 minutes.

SAUTÉ: Heat 1 tablespoon oil in a large pot over medium-high heat. Add the onion and salt. Cover and cook until softened, 5 minutes. Stir occasionally. Add the bell pepper and cook, stirring occasionally, until the pepper is tender, 5 minutes. Remove the vegetables and set aside. Heat the remaining 1 tablespoon oil in the pot and add the seitan. Cook, stirring occasionally, until golden brown, about 5 minutes. Strain the au jus into the pot and add the spinach. Cook until the liquid evaporates, about 2 minutes. To serve, divide the tater tots among 4 bowls, divide the vegetables over the tater tots, divide the seitan over the vegetables, and top with cheese sauce.

 QUICK TIPS: Start by heating the water for the cashews and the broth for the *au jus*. Once the cashews and broth are cooking, chop the onion. While the onion cooks, chop the bell pepper. While the bell pepper cooks, chop the seitan. To chop the seitan, place the palm of your hand on top of the seitan and carefully cut it at a deep angle on the bias.

chickpea brasoi bowl

SERVES 4 | GF, SF

This is a dish of fried potatoes and meat tossed in a paprika-garlic sauce. I still recall how much I loved this dish as a young child, but even then I was picking out the potato pieces as my favorite bites. My version of brasoi keeps intact the delicious paprika sauce, but skips on frying the potatoes. This is just as good as I remember.

POTATOES

- 1 1/2 pounds Yukon God or other waxy potatoes, peeled and cut into 1/2-inch dice
- 1/2 small onion, finely grated
- 1 tablespoon olive oil
- 1/2 teaspoon sea salt
- Black pepper, to taste
- 1/4 cup vegetable broth

BEANS

- 1 tablespoon olive oil
- 2 cups cooked chickpeas

SAUCE

- 1 tablespoon olive oil
- 10 garlic cloves, minced
- 1 1/2 tablespoons Hungarian paprika
- 1/2 cup vegetable broth

SALAD

- 1 medium cucumber, sliced paper-thin
- 1 bell pepper, sliced paper-thin
- 1/2 small onion, sliced paper-thin
- 1 garlic clove, finely minced
- 2 tablespoons white wine vinegar
- 2 tablespoons water
- 1 teaspoon natural sugar
- 1/2 teaspoon sea salt

POTATOES: Combine the potatoes, onion, oil, salt and pepper in a large bowl. Heat a large skillet over medium-high heat and add the potatoes. Cook, stirring, until the potatoes are golden brown, about 6 minutes. Add the broth, cover and cook until tender, about 6 minutes, stirring occasionally.

BEANS: Heat the oil in a large pot over medium heat. Add the chickpeas and cook, stirring, until golden brown. Transfer to a bowl and set aside.

SAUCE: Heat the oil in the now empty large pot over medium heat. Add the garlic and cook until golden, about 1 minute. Add the paprika and vegetable broth. Stir well, bring to simmer and add the reserved potatoes and chickpeas. Stir gently. Taste and adjust seasoning with salt and black pepper

SALAD: Combine the cucumber, bell pepper, onion, garlic, vinegar, water, sugar and salt in a medium bowl. To serve, drain the salad. Spoon the brasoi into bowls, and serve topped with the salad.

QUICK TIPS: Make the salad while the potatoes cook.

puttanesca bowl with sautéed kale (page 72)

five | pasta bowls

Pasta tends to be the go-to vegan meal. I'm sure I'm not the only one who makes a tomato-based pasta dish almost every week. I also get a hankering for pasta served in different ways with deeper flavors, different textures, and a wider variety of sauces. That's when I start yearning for something exotic, like Indonesian Stir-Fried Noodles or a vegan Mushroom Carbonara. The pasta bowls in this chapter are as varied as can be, from Asian and Italian pastas to the essential vegan mac and cheese. Every cookbook needs a vegan mac and cheese, and I bring you two variations. Get your pot of salted water on the stove over high heat before you start making the recipes in this chapter, because the sauces will be done that fast.

veggie lasagna bowl

Assembling a traditional lasagna takes a bit of work, but this bowl dish will have you cooking it up in no time. Just like the casserole-style version, this dish contains everything that is great about lasagna: noodles, sauce, vegetables, and a creamy vegan ricotta.

SAUCE

- 2 medium carrots, cut into large chunks
- 1 medium onion, cut into large chunks
- 3 garlic cloves
- 1 tablespoon olive oil
- 2 teaspoons dried basil
- 1 teaspoon dried oregano
- 1/4 teaspoon red pepper flakes
- 1 teaspoon sea salt
- 4 cups diced ripe tomatoes
- 2 cups water
- 8 ounces curly-edged lasagna noodles, broken into about 2-inch pieces

VEGETABLES

- 1 tablespoon olive oil
- 1 medium zucchini, cut into 1/2-inch dice (3 cups)
- Sea salt and black pepper, to taste
- 6 cups baby spinach (about 5 ounces)
- 1 cup shredded vegan cheese (optional)

TOFU

- 1/4 cup blanched whole almonds
- 1 garlic clove
- 7-ounces super-firm tofu, rinsed
- 2 scallions, coarsely chopped
- 1 teaspoon dried basil
- 1/2 teaspoon sea salt
- Black pepper, to taste

SUBSTITUTION: Substitute firm or extra-firm tofu, pressed for about an hour, for the super firm tofu. Substitute 1 (28-ounce) can diced tomatoes, lightly drained, for the fresh tomatoes.

SAUCE: Combine the carrots, onion, and garlic in a food processor. Process until finely chopped. Heat the oil in a large pot over medium-high heat. Add the minced vegetables, basil, oregano, red pepper flakes, and salt. Cover and cook until softened, about 3 minutes. Stir in the tomatoes, water, and noodles. Cover and bring to boil, then reduce the heat to medium and cook until the pasta is tender, about 15 minutes.

VEGETABLES: Heat the oil in a large skillet over medium heat. Add the zucchini, salt, and black pepper and cook, uncovered, stirring occasionally, until golden, 6 to 8 minutes.

TOFU: Wipe out the food processor and add the almonds and garlic. Process until finely ground. Add the tofu, scallions, basil, salt, and black pepper. Process until smooth and set aside.

ASSEMBLY: Taste the sauce and adjust the seasoning, if needed. Add the zucchini and spinach. Stir well, add the optional cheese, drop tablespoons of tofu mixture onto the sauce, cover and cook until heated through, about 2 minutes. Serve in bowls.

QUICK TIPS: Chop the tomatoes while the carrots cook. Break the noodles while the sauce comes to a boil. Make the tofu while the zucchini cooks.

indonesian stir-fried noodle bowl

SERVES 4 | GF

Mei goreng or bami goreng is a popular street food all over Indonesia, Malaysia, and Singapore. It is a sweet and spicy dish of noodles fried with vegetables and eggs. The sauce usually calls for *kecap manis,* a thick, sweet sauce, but here we will make our own sauce using tamari, mirin, fresh ginger, and garlic.

NOODLES

8 ounces medium-thickness brown rice noodles

SAUCE

1/4 cup vegetable broth

1/4 cup reduced-sodium tamari

1/4 cup mirin

1 tablespoon sambal oelek, or to taste

1 teaspoon grated ginger

1 teaspoon minced garlic

1/4 teaspoon natural sugar

VEGETABLES

1/4 cup vegetable broth, divided

1 small red onion, cut into 1/8-inch slices

3 cups small broccoli florets

3 cups finely shredded cabbage

1 celery rib, cut into 1/8-inch slices

4 garlic cloves, minced

2 tablespoons grapeseed oil or vegetable broth

6 ounces baby kale or baby spinach

1 cup frozen shelled edamame, thawed in a bowl of hot water and drained

SUBSTITUTIONS: Substitute thawed frozen lima beans for the edamame. Substitute sriracha for the sambal oelek.

NOODLES: Bring a medium saucepan of water to boil. Add the noodles and cook just shy of al dente, stirring frequently, about 3 minutes. Drain the noodles and cool under running water. Set aside.

SAUCE: Combine the broth, tamari, mirin, sambal oelek, ginger, garlic, and sugar in a small bowl. Set aside.

VEGETABLES: Heat a large skillet over medium-high heat. Add 1 tablespoon of broth and the onion. Stir and cook until the onion is browned, about 5 minutes. Remove from the skillet and set aside in a medium bowl.

Add 1 tablespoon of broth to the skillet. Add the broccoli. Stir and cook until the broccoli begins to char, about 2 minutes. Add the cabbage, celery, garlic and 1 tablespoon of broth. Stir and cook until the cabbage begins to char, about 2 more minutes. Remove from skillet and set aside with the onion.

Add the sauce to the skillet and simmer until reduced by half, about 2 minutes. Add the oil or 2 more tablespoons of broth, the kale, the edamame, the reserved noodles, and the reserved vegetables. Stir and cook until the pasta is warmed through and beginning to brown, about 4 minutes. Taste and adjust seasoning with more sambal oelek and tamari. Serve hot in bowls.

QUICK TIPS: Heat the water for the noodles first then chop the vegetables while the noodle water comes to a boil. Make the sauce while the pasta cooks. Prepare all the stir-fry ingredients before beginning to cook. You will need a total of 6 cloves of garlic, minced, for the sauce and the stir-fry. Use a nonstick skillet or remove the noodles from the pan as soon as they begin to stick to the bottom.

mushroom carbonara bowl

SERVES 4 | GFO, SFO

After closing, a restaurant staff usually wants something to eat, so the cooks come up with simple family-style dishes that use readily available ingredients. This is how mushroom carbonara came to be. Veganizing the original carbonara recipe takes a few steps, but the result is a creamy pasta dish complete with vegan bacon.

10 ounces linguine

MUSHROOMS

12 ounces shiitake mushrooms, wiped clean, tough stems removed, sliced very thin

2 tablespoons reduced-sodium tamari

1 tablespoon olive oil

2 teaspoons smoked paprika

SAUCE

2/3 cup raw cashew pieces

1/2 cup water

3 garlic cloves

1 tablespoon white miso

VEGETABLES

1/4 cup white wine or dry vermouth

6 cups baby spinach (about 5 ounces)

1/2 cup reserved pasta cooking water

1 cup frozen green peas, rinsed to thaw

1 teaspoon fresh ground black pepper

4 scallions, minced

Indian black salt (optional)

GLUTEN-FREE OPTION: Use gluten-free pasta.

SOY-FREE OPTION: Substitute coconut aminos with 1/8 teaspoon sea salt for the tamari. Substitute chickpea miso for the white miso.

Bring a large pot of salted water to boil over high heat. Add the linguine and cook 1 minute shy of al dente. Drain, reserving 1 cup of pasta cooking water. Transfer the pasta back to the pot and set aside.

MUSHROOMS: Preheat the oven to 425°F. Spread the mushrooms evenly on a large baking sheet. Bake until the mushrooms shrink considerably, 5 to 8 minutes. Combine the tamari, oil and paprika in a small bowl, mixing well. Add the mixture to the mushrooms and stir well. Spread the mushrooms out as much as possible and continue to bake until almost crisp, about 15 minutes, stirring midway through baking.

SAUCE: Combine the cashews with enough water to cover in a small saucepan. Cover the pan, bring to boil, reduce to simmer and cook for 5 minutes. Remove from the heat and set aside for 5 minutes. Drain the cashews, rinse well and transfer to a blender. Add the water, garlic, and miso. Blend until smooth.

ASSEMBLY: Heat the pasta over medium heat and add the wine and cashew mixture, stirring well. Cook until the sauce thickens, about 2 minutes. Add the spinach, 1/2 cup of the reserved cooking water, and peas. Stir well and cook until the spinach wilts, about 2 minutes. Add more pasta water a little at a time if the sauce is too thick. Taste and adjust seasoning. Serve the pasta in shallow bowls, garnished with lots of black pepper, scallions, mushrooms, and black salt, if using.

QUICK TIPS: First, preheat the oven to 425°F, then heat the water for the pasta and cashews. While the water comes to a boil and the oven preheats, slice the mushrooms. Use your kitchen timer consistently for timing the pasta, oven, and cashews. Rinse the cashews and the peas using a strainer.

lemongrass bok choy and tofu bowl

SERVES 4 | GFO

Lemongrass has a wonderfully subtle citrus flavor without the acid that typically accompanies citrus fruits. The creamy sauce for this pasta dish brings a light lemony flavor to the senses. The tofu itself is accented with lemon zest. The lemon is delicate in this dish, which is just perfect with the bok choy.

SAUCE

- 1 cup raw cashew pieces
- 1 teaspoon grapeseed oil
- 4 garlic cloves, minced
- 3 stalks lemongrass, minced (see below)
- 2 teaspoons grated ginger
- 1/4 teaspoon red pepper flakes
- 1 1/2 cups water
- 1 tablespoon white miso

PASTA

- 12 ounces bite-sized pasta such as elbows or penne
- Sea salt and black pepper
- 2 teaspoons fresh lemon juice

TOFU

- 3 tablespoons organic cornstarch or arrowroot
- Zest of 1 lemon
- 1/2 teaspoon sea salt
- 1 (14-ounce) package super-firm tofu, rinsed and cut into 3/4-inch dice
- 2 tablespoons grapeseed oil
- 8 cups chopped bok choy or napa cabbage

GLUTEN-FREE OPTION: Use gluten-free pasta.

SUBSTITUTION: Substitute firm or extra-firm tofu, pressed for about an hour, for the super firm tofu.

PREPARING LEMONGRASS: Cut off the bottom 2 inches of the stalk. Cut off the top 4 to 6 inches of the papery stalk. Remove and discard 2 or 3 tough outer leaves. Cut the remaining stalk into 2 3-inch long pieces. Using a rolling pin, smash the pieces to release the flavor and break up the tough fibers. Mince the smashed stalks.

SAUCE: Combine the cashews with enough water to cover in a medium saucepan. Cover, bring to a boil, reduce to a simmer, and cook for 5 minutes. Remove from heat and set aside for 5 minutes. Drain the cashews, rinse well and transfer to a blender.

Heat the oil in the medium saucepan over medium heat. Add the garlic, lemongrass, ginger and red pepper flakes. Cook until the garlic is golden, about 1 minute, and add the water. Simmer over medium heat for 10 minutes. Add the lemongrass broth and miso to the blender and blend well. Set aside.

PASTA: Heat a large pot of salted water to boil. Add the pasta and cook over medium heat until the pasta is 1 minute shy of al dente. Reserve 2 cups of the cooking water, drain the pasta and return to the pot. Using a fine-mesh strainer, strain the blended sauce into the pasta, using the back of a large spoon to help push the sauce through, return the pasta to simmer and add 1 cup of the reserved pasta water. Cook, stirring often, until the pasta is tender and the sauce is thickened. Add more reserved water to thin, if needed. Taste and adjust seasoning with salt and pepper. Stir in the lemon juice.

TOFU: Combine the cornstarch, zest and salt in a medium bowl. Toss the tofu with the cornstarch mixture. Heat the oil in a large skillet over medium-high heat. Add the tofu and cook until golden brown on all sides, 8 to 10 minutes. Transfer to a bowl and set aside.

Add the bok choy to the skillet and cook until seared, about 3 minutes, stirring as needed. Serve the pasta in bowls with the tofu and bok choy.

QUICK TIPS: First, heat the water for the pasta and cashews, then chop all ingredients while the cashews are cooking and soaking. Zest the lemon before juicing it.

braised butternut bowl
with sage and chard

SERVES 4 | GFO, SFO

The classic pairing of butternut squash and sage make an appearance in this pasta dish. All the flavor notes are played here: sweetness from the squash and pecans, earthiness from the chard, and a little heat from the red pepper flakes. The crowning glory is the fried sage that is crumbled on the finished dish.

PASTA

12 ounces penne

8 ounces chard, tough stems removed and
    coarsely chopped

2 cups cooked pinto beans

BASE

1 teaspoon olive oil

1 cup raw whole pecans

12 to 16 whole sage leaves (not dried sage)

1 teaspoon toasted sesame oil

1 small onion, cut into 1/8-inch thick half moons

1/2 teaspoon red pepper flakes

SAUCE

1 teaspoon olive oil

2 pounds butternut squash (about 1 medium),
    peeled, seeded and cut into 1-inch cubes

1 cup vegetable broth

1 cup reserved pasta cooking water

1 tablespoon white miso

1 teaspoon white wine vinegar

1/4 teaspoon fresh ground nutmeg

Sea salt and black pepper

GLUTEN-FREE OPTION: Use gluten-free pasta.

SOY-FREE OPTION: Substitute chickpea miso for the white miso.

PASTA: Bring a large pot of salted water to boil over high heat. Add the pasta and cook until 4 minutes shy of al dente. Using a ladle, scoop out 1 cup of cooking water and set aside for the sauce. Add the chard and cook two minutes. Add the beans and cook 1 more minute. Drain, return to the pot and keep warm.

BASE: Heat the olive oil in a large pot over medium heat. Add the pecans and cook until toasted, about 3 minutes, stirring frequently. Remove from the pot and set aside in a small bowl. Add the sage and cook until crisp, about 1 minute. Remove the sage and set aside with the nuts. Add the sesame oil and onion, cover and cook until softened, about 3 minutes, stirring occasionally. Remove and set aside in a separate small bowl.

SAUCE: Add the oil and squash and cook until golden brown, about 8 minutes, stirring occasionally. Add the broth, the reserved onion, and four of the sage leaves, crumbled. Cover and cook until fork-tender, about 5 more minutes, stirring occasionally.

Combine the reserved pasta water with the miso and vinegar, mixing well. Add the miso mixture to the squash. Add the nutmeg and season with salt and black pepper. Add the reserved pasta-bean mixture, stir, and adjust seasoning. Cook until the pasta is al dente and the flavors have melded. Coarsely chop the pecan and sage mixture. Transfer the pasta mixture to bowls and top with the pecan and sage mixture.

 QUICK TIPS: Slice the onion and peel and seed the squash before you begin toasting the nuts. Cut off both ends of the squash before you begin peeling with a vegetable peeler. Use an ice cream scooper to remove the seeds of the squash. Chop the squash while the nuts and onion are cooking.

hungarian lecsó pasta bowl with seitan

SERVES 4 | GFO, SF

Lecsó is the most essential component of a truly great Hungarian dish. It might seem a simple matter of cooking up some onion, bell pepper, and tomato, but the process of cooking it is where the flavor is; each component of the lecsó needs to be added at a different time, giving the previous ingredient a chance to cook down. This is not just another tomato-based pasta dish.

LECSÓ

2 tablespoons grapeseed oil

2 medium onions, cut into 1/4-inch thick half moons

2 large green or red bell peppers, cut into 1/4-inch thick slices

4 large Roma tomatoes, coarsely chopped

1 tablespoon Hungarian paprika

Sea salt and black pepper

PASTA

8 ounces spaghetti

8 ounces kale, tough stems removed, coarsely chopped

SEITAN

1/4 cup whole-wheat pastry flour or all-purpose flour

1/2 teaspoon Hungarian paprika

Sea salt and black pepper

1 pound Slow-Simmered Seitan (page 11) or store-bought, cut into 1/2 inch thick slices

1 tablespoon grapeseed oil

GLUTEN-FREE OPTION: Substitute fried tofu or 3 cups of sautéed cauliflower or an assortment of vegetables for the seitan. Use a gluten-free pasta.

LECSÓ: Heat the oil in the large pot over medium heat. Add the onion, cover and cook until softened, about 5 minutes. Add the bell pepper, cover and cook until the pepper softens, 5 more minutes. Add the tomato and cook, uncovered, until the lecsó is cooked down, about 10 more minutes. Add the paprika, season with salt and black pepper and cook for another 5 minutes.

PASTA: Bring a large pot of salted water to boil over high heat. Add the pasta, reduce to medium, and cook until 4 minutes shy of al dente. Add the kale and cook until the pasta and kale are tender. Drain, return to the pot and set aside.

SEITAN: Combine the flour and paprika in a medium bowl. Season with salt and black pepper and toss with the seitan. Heat the oil in a large skillet over medium-high heat. Add the seitan and cook until almost crisp, about 4 minutes. Do this in batches to avoid crowding the skillet. Remove from the skillet and set aside.

ASSEMBLY: Add the pasta and kale to the lecsó and cook for 2 more minutes to meld the flavors. Serve in shallow bowls topped with the seitan.

QUICK TIPS: To begin, heat the water for the pasta. Chop the peppers while the onions are cooking. Chop the tomatoes while the peppers cook. Prepare the kale while the tomatoes cook. Preheat the skillet to ensure a good sear on the seitan.

puttanesca bowl
with sautéed kale

SERVES 4 | GFO, SFO

Puttanesca is probably my favorite red sauce for pasta. It is a pungent, salty tomato-based sauce with olives, capers, and spice. Most puttanesca recipes include anchovies, but in this wonderful vegan version, white miso has the triple duty of bringing a unique saltiness, a sharp-cheesy flavor, and a fermented umami flavor to the dish that anchovies are credited with supplying. (See photo on page 60.)

PASTA

12 ounces spaghetti

SAUCE

2 tablespoons olive oil

1/4 to 1 teaspoon red pepper flakes

1 cup pitted Kalamata olives, drained and coarsely chopped, divided

2 tablespoons red wine

2 (15-ounce) cans diced tomatoes, drained and juices reserved

3 tablespoons capers, drained and rinsed

2 tablespoons white miso

Black pepper

KALE

1 tablespoon olive oil

4 garlic cloves, minced

1 pound kale, tough stems removed, chopped

SOY-FREE OPTION: Substitute chickpea miso for the white miso.

GLUTEN-FREE OPTION: Use gluten-free pasta.

PASTA: Bring a large pot of salted water to boil. Add the spaghetti and cook 1 minute shy of al dente. Drain and set aside.

SAUCE: Heat the oil in a large pot over medium-high heat. Add the red pepper flakes and half of the olives. Cook for 1 minute. Add the red wine and cook until the wine evaporates, about 1 minute. Add the diced tomatoes and capers. Bring to boil, reduce to simmer and cook over medium heat until the sauce thickens and the tomatoes break down, about 10 minutes.

Combine the reserved tomato juice and miso, stirring well using a small whisk or fork. Add the miso mixture, the pasta, and remaining olives to the sauce, mixing well. Season with salt and black pepper. Cook until the pasta is tender, about 2 minutes.

KALE: Heat the oil in a large skillet over medium-high heat. Add the garlic and cook until fragrant, about 30 seconds. Add the kale, stirring well with tongs. Cover and cook until tender, about 4 minutes, stirring occasionally. Serve the pasta in bowls, garnished with the kale.

QUICK TIPS: Begin preparing the sauce while the pasta water comes to a boil. Remember to set the timer for the pasta. Chop the kale while the sauce cooks.

lemon-caper cannellini couscous bowl

SERVES 4 | SF

This is another delicately flavored lemony dish, but in this case the more assertive capers bring a depth that is distinctive. Israeli couscous is also known as pearled couscous, and the pasta is much larger than the regular small-grained couscous. If you have preserved lemon, it is an excellent accompaniment to this light dish.

COUSCOUS

2 cups water

1/2 teaspoon sea salt

1 1/2 cups Israeli couscous

SAUTÉ

1 tablespoon olive oil

1/2 medium onion, finely chopped

4 garlic cloves, minced

1 tablespoon whole wheat pastry or all-purpose flour

1/2 cup white wine or dry vermouth

1/4 teaspoon red pepper flakes

SAUCE

1 cup vegetable broth

1 tablespoon fresh lemon juice

2 cups cooked cannellini beans

8 ounces chard, tough stems removed, coarsely chopped

2 tablespoons drained capers

1 tablespoon minced preserved lemons, rinsed, plain and not sweet or spiced (optional)

1 tablespoon minced parsley

Salt and black pepper, to taste

Lemon slices

COUSCOUS: Heat the water and salt in a medium saucepan over high heat. Bring to boil. Add the couscous, cover, reduce to simmer and cook until it is tender and the water is absorbed, about 10 minutes. Set aside.

SAUTÉ: Heat the oil in a large skillet over medium heat. Stir in the onion and garlic. Cover and cook, stirring occasionally, until the onions are golden, about 6 minutes. Stir in the flour and cook for one minute. Stir in the wine and red pepper flakes and cook until the wine evaporates.

SAUCE: Stir in the broth, lemon juice, beans, chard, capers, and the preserved lemons, if using. Cover and cook until the chard wilts, about 2 minutes. Uncover and cook until the sauce reduces by half, about 4 minutes.

Stir in the parsley and reserved couscous. Season to taste with salt and black pepper and cook until heated through, about 1 minute. Taste and adjust seasoning. Serve in bowls with lemon slices.

 QUICK TIPS: Chop the chard and parsley before making the sauté.

reuben mac and cheese bowl

SERVES 4 | GFO, SFO

The classic Reuben gets another makeover! This time the popular sandwich reincarnates as macaroni and cheese. All the best parts of the Reuben are here, including the sauerkraut and rye bread. It has become one of our favorite ways to enjoy a Reuben.

PASTA

8 ounces pasta, such as elbows, shells, or penne

2 cups sauerkraut, lightly rinsed and drained

1/2 teaspoon caraway seeds

SAUCE

1/2 cup raw cashew pieces

1/2 small onion, coarsely chopped

1 garlic clove

3 tablespoons coarsely chopped jarred roasted red pepper

3/4 cup unsweetened plain nondairy milk

2 tablespoons white miso

1 tablespoon tahini

1/2 teaspoon sea salt

TOFU

3 tablespoons grapeseed oil

1 (14-ounce) package super-firm tofu, rinsed

Sea salt a black pepper

2 tablespoons drained capers, patted dry

CRUMBS

1 tablespoon grapeseed oil (optional)

1 cup rye bread crumbs

GLUTEN-FREE OPTION: Use gluten-free pasta and gluten-free bread for the crumbs.

SOY-FREE OPTION: Substitute chickpea miso for the white miso. Replace the tofu with 8 ounces of seitan cut into 1/4-inch pieces.

SUBSTITUTION: Substitute firm or extra-firm tofu, pressed for about an hour, for the super firm tofu.

PASTA: Heat a medium saucepan of salted water to boiling. Cook the pasta until al dente. Drain, return to the pan and set aside.

SAUCE: Combine the cashews and enough water to cover in a small saucepan over high heat. Cover, bring to boil, reduce to simmer and cook for 5 minutes. Remove from heat and set aside for 5 minutes. Drain the cashews, rinse, and transfer to a blender. Add the onion, garlic, red pepper, milk, miso, tahini and salt. Blend until very smooth.

Add the sauce to the cooked pasta along with the sauerkraut and caraway seeds. Cook over medium heat until the sauce is thick and everything is heated through, about 3 minutes.

TOFU: Heat the oil in a large skillet over medium heat. Cut the tofu in 1/2-inch slices lengthwise. Cook the tofu in the oil until crisp, about 4 minutes per side. Transfer to paper towels to drain; season with salt and pepper. Cut the tofu into 1/2-inch wide pieces. Add the capers to the hot oil and cook until crisp, about 2 minutes. Take care when adding the capers as they will sputter the oil. Have a lid handy and cover the pan partly until the water evaporates. Remove the capers with a slotted spoon and drain on paper towels.

CRUMBS: Add the oil to the skillet, if needed, and add the bread crumbs. Cook, stirring, until golden and crisp. Serve the mac and cheese in bowls topped with the tofu and fried capers.

 QUICK TIPS: Begin by heating the water for the pasta and the cashews. Prepare the sauce ingredients while the cashews soak. To make rye bread crumbs, process 2 pieces of rye bread in a food processor until coarsely ground.

tex-mex pasta bowl
with pintos and broccoli

SERVES 4 | GFO, SF

This fusion of Mexican and Texan flavors is like combining the best of both worlds. Since Mexico and Texas border each other, it comes as no surprise that elements from each region have intermingled and developed into their own signature flavors.

PASTA

6 cups water

1 teaspoon cumin seeds

Sea salt

8 ounces rotini or fusilli

4 cups broccoli florets

SAUCE

1 cup unsweetened plain nondairy milk

3 tablespoons masa harina

2 teaspoons white miso

2 teaspoons Chipotle Purée (page 14)

1/2 teaspoon mild chili powder

1/2 cup reserved pasta cooking water

BASE

1 tablespoon grapeseed oil

1 medium onion, finely chopped

2 garlic cloves, minced

2 medium ripe tomatoes, coarsely chopped

1 teaspoon dried oregano

2 cups cooked pinto or black beans

Sea salt and black pepper

1 cup shredded vegan cheese (optional)

1/4 cup minced cilantro

GLUTEN-FREE OPTION: Use gluten-free pasta.

PASTA: Heat the water and cumin in a medium saucepan over high heat. Add salt to taste, bring to boil and add the pasta. Add the broccoli when the pasta is 2 minutes shy of al dente. Cook the pasta until al dente. Drain, reserving 1/2 cup of the cooking water. Set aside.

SAUCE: Combine the milk, masa harina, miso, chipotle, and chili powder in a small bowl. Whisk well to combine. Add the reserved pasta cooking water and set aside.

BASE: Heat the oil over medium heat in a large pot. Add the onion, cover and cook until golden, about 7 minutes, stirring occasionally. Add the garlic and cook until fragrant, about 1 minute. Add the tomato and oregano and stir and cook until the tomato breaks down, about 2 minutes.

ASSEMBLY: Stir in the drained pasta, beans, and reserved sauce, and season with salt and pepper. Simmer until the sauce thickens and the broccoli is tender, about 4 minutes, stirring occasionally. Add the cheese, if using. Cover, and cook until the cheese melts and the flavors have melded, about 2 more minutes. Serve in bowls garnished with the cilantro.

QUICK TIPS: Chop the broccoli and onion while the pasta cooks. Make the sauce and chop the tomato while the onion cooks. Chop the cilantro while the pasta finishes cooking.

mushroom larb bowl with rice noodles

SERVES 4 | GF, SFO

Known as the national dish of Laos, larb is traditionally an appetizer of minced meat or mushrooms with fish sauce, mint, and lots of lime. The flavor is unique, a mixture of sour and mint. The uncooked rice is toasted, ground, and sprinkled on the dish before serving. Here I have transformed the popular appetizer into a pasta bowl.

RICE

3 tablespoons uncooked rice

2 teaspoons red pepper flakes

MUSHROOMS

2 tablespoons grapeseed oil, divided

1 pound mushrooms, any kind, wiped clean and minced (gills scraped out, if using portobello)

1/2 small red onion, cut into 1/8-inch thick slices

1/2 cup raw cashew pieces

PASTA

4 ounces thin rice noodles (mei fun)

Hot water

SAUCE

1/4 cup fresh lime juice

2 tablespoons reduced-sodium tamari

2 teaspoons jarred caper brine liquid

2 teaspoons natural sugar

1/4 teaspoon sea salt

3 scallions, minced, divided

1/4 cup coarsely chopped cilantro, divided

1 cup coarsely chopped mint leaves, divided

VEGETABLES

2 cups finely shredded cabbage

1 medium carrot, cut into julienne slices

1/2 medium cucumber, cut into 1/4-inch half-moons

Lime wedges

4 small fresh Thai chiles or 1 small serrano chile, minced (optional)

SOY-FREE OPTION: Substitute coconut aminos and a few punches of sea salt for the tamari.

RICE: Preheat a large skillet over medium heat. Add the rice and cook until toasted, stirring often, about 3 minutes. Transfer to a small blender, add the red pepper flakes and process until finely ground. Set aside.

MUSHROOMS: Heat 2 teaspoons of oil in the large skillet over medium-high heat. Add half of the mushrooms and cook until seared, about 4 minutes. Remove and set aside in a medium bowl. Repeat with 2 teaspoons of oil and the remaining mushrooms and set aside. Heat the remaining 2 teaspoons oil in the skillet and add the onions and cashews. Cook until the cashews are golden and the onion is crisp-tender, about 1 minute. Set aside with the mushrooms.

PASTA: Soak the rice noodles in hot water in a medium bowl until tender, about 2 minutes. Stir well to remove extra starch. Drain and set aside in a separate bowl.

SAUCE: Combine the lime juice, tamari, brine liquid, sugar, and salt in a small bowl. Mix well to dissolve the sugar. Add 2 tablespoons of the sauce to the mushroom mixture along with half of the scallions, half of the cilantro, and half of the mint. Add 2 tablespoons of the sauce to the noodles and mix well.

ASSEMBLY: Divide the pasta and mushroom mixture among four bowls. Divide the cabbage, carrot, and cucumber among the bowls. Garnish the bowls with the remaining scallions, herbs, the ground rice, lime wedges, and chiles, if using. Serve the remaining sauce with the bowls.

QUICK TIPS: Begin by heating the water for the noodles in a medium pot or kettle. Mince the mushrooms in the food processor while the rice toasts. Prepare the other vegetables as you have time, shredding the carrot and cabbage in the food processor, if desired.

wide noodle and collard bowl
with wild mushroom ragout

SERVES 4 | GFO, SF

Wild mushrooms are absolutely delicious in this dish, but even using common mushrooms provide tasty results. Since vegan wide noodles may be more difficult to find, the recipe calls for lasagna noodles. If you do have access to vegan wide noodles, grab a box and cook up a bowl of ragout.

PASTA
- 10 ounces lasagna noodles, broken into 2-inch pieces
- 8 ounces collard greens, tough stems removed, coarsely chopped

MUSHROOMS
- 2 cups vegetable broth
- 1 ounce dried porcini mushrooms
- 1 1/2 tablespoons olive oil
- 1 medium onion, chopped
- 1 tablespoon fresh rosemary
- 6 garlic cloves, minced
- 1 pound fresh mushrooms, any kind, wiped clean and cut into bite-size pieces
- Sea salt and black pepper

SAUCE
- 2 tablespoons tomato paste
- 2 tablespoons dry white wine or sherry
- 1/2 cup minced parsley

GLUTEN-FREE OPTION: Use gluten-free pasta.

PASTA: Bring a large pot of salted water to boil over high heat. Add the pasta and the collards and cook until both are tender. Drain, return to the pot and keep warm.

MUSHROOMS: Combine the broth and porcini in a small saucepan over high heat. Cover and bring to boil, reduce to simmer, and cook for 3 minutes. Remove from heat and set aside for 10 minutes to soften. Drain the porcini, reserving the broth, and rinse the mushrooms in a fine-mesh strainer. If needed, chop the porcinis and set aside. Strain the broth using a coffee filter or reusable tea bag. Set aside.

Heat the oil in a separate large pot over medium heat. Add the onion and rosemary, cover and cook until golden, about 5 minutes, stirring occasionally. Add the garlic and cook for 1 minute. Increase the heat to high and add the fresh mushrooms, season with salt and pepper and cook, stirring occasionally, until mushrooms are golden, about 6 minutes. Reduce heat to medium and add the reserved porcini. Remove the mushrooms and set aside.

SAUCE: Add the tomato paste to the now empty pot and cook, stirring, until it darkens, about 1 minute. Add the wine and cook, stirring, until it evaporates. Add the reserved porcini broth and cook until reduced by half, about 4 minutes. Add the sauce, reserved mushrooms, and parsley to the pasta. Stir well, adjust seasoning, and serve in deep bowls.

QUICK TIPS: First, heat the water for the pasta and the broth for the porcini. Clean and chop the collards while the water heats. Chop the onion and mushrooms while the porcini soaks. If using portobellos, scrape out the gills using a spoon before chopping.

tempeh bowl with fennel sofrito
and sweet potato mofongo
(page 102)

six | grilled bowls

Grilling is an easy, quick, and low-fat cooking method that adds extra flavor to foods. I recommend using a well-seasoned cast iron grill pan for it's non-stick quality. A nonstick electric grill may be used instead. During the summer months, or whenever the mood strikes, grilling outdoors on a charcoal or gas grill is the best way to go, but for convenience and ease, nothing beats a stovetop or electric grill. You can even use a cast iron grill pan to smoke plant proteins, such as in the Jerk Tofu with Coconut Rice recipe. So, preheat your grill pan and get dinner cooking!

sausage-style tofu bowl
with squash and potatoes

SERVES 4 | GF, SFO

Grilling tofu firms up the texture and adds a subtle smokiness. The tofu is first tossed in a flavorful sauce, which is then turned into a light vinaigrette that coats the vegetables and tofu. This is a particularly pretty dish with shades of green, white, and orange.

VEGETABLES

- 1 garlic clove, crushed
- 4 teaspoons dried oregano
- 1 teaspoon red pepper flakes
- 3 bay leaves
- 2 teaspoons sea salt
- 1 1/2 pounds fingerling potatoes, cut lengthwise in half
- 8 ounces Brussels sprouts, trimmed and halved
- 8 ounces butternut squash, peeled, seeded, and cut into 1-inch cubes

VINAIGRETTE

- 6 tablespoons olive oil
- 5 tablespoons vegetable broth
- 2 garlic cloves, crushed
- 1 teaspoon dried basil
- 1 teaspoon sea salt
- Black pepper, to taste
- 3 tablespoons white balsamic vinegar or white wine vinegar

GRILL

- 1 (14-ounce) package firm or extra-firm tofu, rinsed and pressed at least 10 minutes and cut into 1/2-inch slices

SOY-FREE OPTION: Substitute 12 ounces of seitan or 2 cups cooked kidney beans for the tofu. Toss the beans with the marinade and sauté until warm in a large skillet over medium heat, about 4 minutes. Grill the squash as well as the sprouts.

VEGETABLES: Combine the garlic, oregano, red pepper flakes and bay leaves in several layers of cheesecloth or muslin bag. Add the spice bag, salt, and potatoes to a large pot. Add just enough water to cover. Bring to a boil and reduce to a simmer. Cook for 8 minutes. Place a steamer basket on top of the potatoes and add the Brussels sprouts to the steamer basket. Cover and cook for 5 minutes. Add the squash to the steamer basket and cook until all the vegetables are tender, about 5 more minutes. Set aside the sprouts and squash. Remove the spice bag, drain the potatoes, and set aside.

VINAIGRETTE: Combine the oil, broth, garlic, basil, salt, and black pepper in a blender. Blend until smooth and transfer to a large bowl. Do not add the vinegar yet.

GRILL: Heat a grill pan over medium heat. Toss the tofu slices in the vinaigrette and grill until marks appear, about 4 minutes per side. Set aside. Toss the steamed sprouts in the vinaigrette and grill them, cut side down, until marks appear, about 2 minutes. Set aside.

ASSEMBLY: Add the vinegar to the remaining dressing in the bowl and whisk to combine. Taste and adjust seasoning. Add the potatoes, sprouts, and squash. Toss to combine. To serve, divide the vegetables among four bowls, top with the grilled tofu and add more vinaigrette as desired. Serve immediately.

QUICK TIPS: First, press the tofu, then heat the water for the potatoes. Chop the sprouts while the potatoes begin cooking. Cut the squash while the sprouts begin to steam. Make the vinaigrette and cut the tofu while the grill pan preheats.

jerk tofu bowl with coconut rice

SERVES 4 | SFO

Authentic jerk is about the seasoning as well as the cooking method: smoking over pimento wood, which has the distinct flavor of allspice berries and bay leaves. In this recipe, we will smoke using fresh bay leaves and dried allspice berries after marinating the tofu with jerk spices. A grill pan, stovetop smoker, or an outdoor grill is essential for this recipe. Smoke the tofu for up to 20 minutes before adding the asparagus for an intense bay flavor.

MARINADE

- 1/4 cup vegetable broth
- 1 tablespoon grapeseed oil
- 1 tablespoon fresh lime juice
- 1 tablespoon reduced-sodium tamari
- 2 teaspoons natural dark sugar
- 2 teaspoons fresh thyme
- 1 teaspoon garlic granules
- 1/2 teaspoon ground allspice
- 1/2 teaspoon sea salt
- 1/2 teaspoon black pepper
- 1/2 to 1 small habanero chile, seeded
- 3 scallions, coarsely chopped
- 1 (1-inch) piece fresh ginger, sliced
- 1 (14-ounce) package super-firm tofu, cut into 1/2-inch slices

RICE

- 1 3/4 cups water
- 1/2 teaspoon sea salt
- 1 cup long-grain white rice
- 1/2 cup dried shredded unsweetened coconut

GRILL

- 1 (3-ounce) package fresh bay leaves
- 2 tablespoons whole allspice berries
- 8 ounces asparagus, trimmed
- Sea salt and black pepper, to taste

SALAD

- 1/4 cup white wine vinegar
- 1 teaspoon grapeseed oil
- 2 teaspoons natural sugar
- 1/4 teaspoon sea salt
- Two pinches allspice and thyme
- Black pepper, to taste
- 1 large cucumber, peeled, seeded, and chopped

MARINADE: In a blender, combine the broth, oil, lime juice, tamari, sugar, thyme, garlic granules, ground allspice, salt, pepper, habanero, scallions, and ginger. Blend as smooth as possible. Rub the marinade into the tofu slices and set aside in a shallow pan while the grill pan preheats, about 4 minutes.

RICE: Heat the water and salt in a medium saucepan over high heat. Rinse the rice in two changes of fresh water and add to the pan along with the dried coconut. When the water is bubbling, cover the pan, reduce the heat to low and cook for 15 minutes. Remove from the heat and set aside for 10 minutes to steam. Fluff with a fork before serving.

GRILL: Heat a grill pan over medium heat. Add the bay leaves in a single layer and scatter the allspice berries over the leaves. Place the marinated tofu slices directly over the bay leaves. Cover the pan tightly with heavy-duty aluminum foil. Smoke over medium heat for 10 minutes. There should be no smoke escaping from the pan, but use a stove fan if there is a little smoke. Uncover one side, add the asparagus, then cover and smoke for another 5 minutes.

After smoking, discard the bay leaves and berries, spray the grill pan with oil, and grill the tofu until grill marks appear, about 2 minutes per side, basting with the remaining marinade. Season with salt and pepper. Grill the asparagus for 1 minute to reheat, if needed.

SALAD: Combine the vinegar, oil, sugar, salt, allspice, and thyme in a medium bowl. Add pepper, to taste. Add the cucumber and toss to combine. Serve the rice in bowls topped with the tofu and asparagus. Drain the salad and place next to the tofu.

SOY-FREE OPTION: Substitute 4 small portobello mushrooms for the tofu. Substitute coconut aminos and a few pinches of sea salt for the tamari.

SUBSTITUTION: Substitute firm or extra-firm tofu, pressed for about an hour, for the super-firm tofu.

QUICK TIPS: First, assemble all marinade ingredients, then heat the water for the rice and preheat the grill pan as it will need about 5 minutes to heat up. Make the salad while the tofu smokes. Use gloves while handling the habanero and the marinade.

chimichurri grilled zucchini-couscous bowl

SERVES 4 | GFO, SF

Chimichurri sauce is originally from Argentina, but, just like any other great thing, the fragrant green sauce has been adapted in multiple cuisines. The sauce is a blend of herbs, garlic, vinegar, and olive oil, but in this recipe I've lightened up on the oil while still retaining all the goodness.

SAUCE

3 tablespoons olive oil

2 teaspoons fresh or dried oregano

1/4 cup white wine vinegar

1/4 cup water

2 tablespoons fresh lime juice

2 cups lightly packed parsley

1 cup lightly packed cilantro

1 medium jalapeño, seeded

8 garlic cloves

Sea salt and black pepper

COUSCOUS

2 cups water

1/2 teaspoon sea salt

1 1/2 cups Israeli couscous

1 teaspoon olive oil

2 cups cooked kidney beans

4 cups baby spinach

Zest of 1 lime

Black pepper, to taste

GRILL

Oil spray

2 medium zucchini, cut lengthwise into 1/2-inch slices

4 scallions

Sea salt and black pepper

1/2 cup toasted and salted pepitas (pumpkin seeds)

GLUTEN-FREE OPTION: Substitute 30-Minute Brown Rice (page 16) for the couscous.

SAUCE: Heat the oil in a small saucepan over medium heat. Add the oregano and cook for 30 seconds. Remove from heat and add the vinegar, water, and lime juice. Transfer to a food processor and add the parsley, cilantro, jalapeño, garlic, salt and pepper. Process until smooth as possible. Set aside.

COUSCOUS: Heat the water and salt in a medium saucepan over high heat. Bring to boil, add the couscous, cover, reduce to simmer and cook until the pasta is tender and the water is absorbed, about 10 minutes. Stir in the oil, beans and spinach. Cover and cook until the spinach is wilted and the beans are heated through, about 2 minutes. Stir in the lime zest and pepper and keep warm.

GRILL: Heat a grill pan over medium heat. Spray the pan with oil and grill the zucchini until tender, about 4 minutes per side, rotating the squash a quarter turn after 2 minutes. Baste the squash with the sauce while cooking. Set aside. Cook the scallions until tender, about 2 minutes per side. Chop the zucchini and scallions into bite-sized pieces. Season with salt and pepper. Serve the couscous in bowls, topped with the grilled vegetables, chimichurri sauce, and pepitas.

SERVING OPTION If you have a few more minutes, cut the squash in half lengthwise and cut into 3/4-inch half-moons. Cut the scallions into 2-inch pieces. Alternatingly skewer the zucchini and scallions onto 4-inch skewers and grill until tender, basting as needed, about 3 minutes per side.

jalapeño bbq tempeh bowl
over creamy grits and chard

SERVES 4 | GF, SFO

Fresh jalapeños are featured twice in this dish: first in the barbecue sauce and then grilled as a garnish. Garnish with the grilled jalapeño to taste, remembering they are spicy even when cooked. The sauce unites the flavors of the tempeh, grits, and chard.

GRITS

- 2 1/2 cups vegetable broth
- 1/2 teaspoon sea salt
- 1 1/4 cups medium-ground corn grits, cornmeal, or polenta (do not use instant)
- 1 1/2 cups unsweetened plain nondairy milk, divided
- Sea salt and black pepper, to taste

SAUCE

- 2 teaspoons grapeseed oil
- 1 small onion, finely chopped
- 1 small jalapeño, seeded and minced
- 4 garlic cloves, minced
- 3/4 cup ketchup
- 1/3 cup water
- 3 tablespoons apple cider vinegar
- 1 1/2 tablespoons molasses
- 1 1/2 tablespoons reduced-sodium tamari
- 1 tablespoon pure maple syrup
- Sea salt and black pepper

VEGETABLES

- 4 cups chopped vegetables (carrot, turnip, sweet potato, squash, green beans, etc.)
- 8 ounces chard, tough stems removed, coarsely chopped
- 1 teaspoon grapeseed oil
- Sea salt and black pepper

GRILL

- 8-ounces tempeh
- 2 small jalapeños
- 1 teaspoon grapeseed oil

GRITS: Combine the broth and salt in a medium saucepan. Cover and bring to boil. Stir in the grits with a whisk. Reduce to simmer over medium heat and cook until thickened, 2 to 5 minutes. Stir in 1 cup of milk and simmer over low heat until the grits are tender, 10 to 15 minutes, partly covered. Stir in the remaining 1/2 cup of milk just before serving if the grits are too thick. Taste and adjust seasoning with salt and pepper. Set aside but keep warm.

SAUCE: Heat the oil in a small saucepan over medium heat. Add the onion, jalapeño, and garlic. Stir and cook until softened, about 4 minutes. Stir in the ketchup, water, vinegar, molasses, tamari, and maple syrup. Bring to boil, reduce to simmer over medium heat and cook until thickened, about 10 minutes. Taste and season with salt and pepper.

VEGETABLES: Prepare a steamer basket in a large pot. Steam the dense vegetables (carrot, turnip, etc.) for 7 minutes. Add the softer vegetables (summer squash, etc.) and continue steaming for 4 minutes, then add the chard. Steam until all the vegetables are tender, about 5 minutes. Drizzle the vegetables with the oil and season with salt and pepper. Keep warm.

GRILL: Heat a grill pan over medium-high heat. Cut the tempeh in half into 2 blocks. Cut each block in half diagonally. Cut each triangle in half through the middle to yield 8 thin triangles of tempeh. Combine the tempeh, jalapeños and oil in a medium bowl. Grill the jalapeños until slightly charred, about 8 minutes, turning as needed. Grill the tempeh triangles for 2 minutes, flip, baste with the sauce and cook for 3 minutes. Flip, baste with the sauce and cook for another 3 minutes.

ASSEMBLY: Divide the grits among 4 bowls. Divide the vegetables among the bowls. Add 2 barbequed tempeh slices to each bowl. Chop the jalapeños and serve with the bowls. Serve with the remaining sauce.

SOY-FREE OPTIONS: Substitute 10 ounces of seitan for the tempeh or 4 large portobello mushrooms. Remove the stems, scrape the gills and cut off the edges of the mushroom to allow for even grilling. Grill the seitan or mushrooms as you would the tempeh. Substitute coconut aminos and a few pinches of sea salt for the tamari.

QUICK TIPS: First, heat the broth for the grits, then measure the grits and chop the onion, jalapeño, and garlic for the sauce while the broth heats. Chop vegetables for steaming while the onion cooks. Heat the water for steaming and preheat the grill pan about 5 minutes before needed.

grilled portobello bowl
with farro and succotash

SERVES 4 | GFO, SF

Succotash is originally a Native American dish consisting of beans and corn. Most likely the dish also contained squash, as the three ingredients are collectively known as the Three Sisters, being companion crops.

FARRO

3 cups vegetable broth

1 cup pearled farro, rinsed well

1 teaspoon sea salt

PORTOBELLO

1/4 cup Marsala wine

1/2 small red onion or 1 shallot, grated

1 tablespoon tomato paste

1 tablespoon olive oil

1 tablespoon fresh rosemary

4 medium portobello mushrooms, wiped clean, stems and gills removed

SUCCOTASH

1 tablespoon olive oil

1 teaspoon fresh rosemary

4 ounces green beans, trimmed, cut into 1-inch pieces

1 yellow summer squash, cut into 1/2-inch dice

1 medium red bell pepper, cut into 1/2-inch dice

1 cup corn kernels, thawed if frozen

8 ounces kale, tough stems removed and minced

Sea salt and black pepper

SAUCE

5 tablespoons vegetable broth

2 tablespoons minced soft sun-dried tomatoes

1 tablespoon olive oil

1 teaspoon Dijon mustard

1 garlic clove

Sea salt and black pepper

GLUTEN-FREE OPTION: Cook 1 cup of rice in the broth instead of farro. (Brown rice will take about 10 minutes longer to cook than farro.)

FARRO: Heat the broth, farro, and salt in a medium pot over high heat. Bring to a boil, reduce to a simmer, and cook until tender, about 20 minutes. Drain, return to the pot and keep warm.

PORTOBELLO: Combine the wine, onion, tomato paste, oil and rosemary in a 9 x 13-inch baking dish. Add the portobello and coat the mushrooms well with the marinade. Marinate the mushrooms until needed.

SUCCOTASH: Heat the oil and rosemary in a large skillet over medium-high heat. Cook for 1 minute to infuse the oil with the herb. Add the beans, squash, bell pepper, corn, and kale. Cover the skillet and cook to wilt, about 2 minutes. Uncover and continue to cook until the beans are tender and the corn is golden, about 7 minutes. Season with salt and pepper.

Preheat a grill pan over medium heat. Grill the mushrooms, basting with the remaining marinade as needed, until tender, about 4 minutes per side, rotating the mushrooms a quarter turn after 2 minutes. Season with salt and pepper.

SAUCE: Combine the broth, tomatoes, oil, mustard, and garlic in a small blender. Blend as smooth as possible, in intervals if needed. Season with salt and pepper. Serve the farro, topped with the succotash, then topped with a mushroom and a drizzle of the sauce in each of 4 bowls.

 QUICK TIPS: Begin by heating the broth for the farro. Chop the vegetables while the skillet preheats. Make the sauce while the succotash cooks. Preheat the grill pan about halfway through the cooking of the succotash. If your sun-dried tomatoes (for the sauce) aren't soft, add the tomatoes to the simmering water for about 4 minutes to soften.

cajun tofu and artichoke bowl

SERVES 4 | GF, SFO

Celery root, or celeriac, tastes like celery, and it can be turned into a sweet, creamy, mild purée. It is the perfect foil for the lightly spicy Cajun tofu. An underused root vegetable, celeriac is a wonderful alternative to mashed potatoes, although mashers or rice may be substituted.

PURÉE

- 5 cups water
- 1 teaspoon sea salt
- 2 pounds celeriac, peeled, cut into 1/2-inch dice
- 1 cup unsweetened plain nondairy milk
- 1 tablespoon olive oil
- Sea salt and black pepper

GRILL

- 2 tablespoons vegetable broth
- 1 tablespoons olive oil
- 1 tablespoon smoked paprika
- 3/4 teaspoon sea salt
- 1/2 teaspoon black pepper
- 1/2 teaspoon dried oregano
- 1/2 teaspoon fresh or dried thyme
- 1/8 to 1/4 teaspoon cayenne
- 2 garlic cloves, finely minced
- 1 (14-ounce package) extra-firm tofu, pressed 10 minutes and cut into 8 (3/4-inch wide) slices

ARTICHOKES

- 1 tablespoon olive oil, plus more for garnish
- 1 (12-ounce) jar artichoke hearts, drained, patted dry, and quartered
- 2 garlic cloves, cut into 1/8-inch slices

SOY-FREE OPTION: Replace the tofu with 4 medium portobello mushrooms. Remove the stem, scrape the gills and cut off the edges to allow for even grilling.

CELERY ROOT (CELERIAC): To peel, cut off the top of the root and place cut-side down on work surface. Use a chef's knife to cut away the tough outer skin. Cut into 1-inch slices and chop as needed. Add the celeriac to boiling water to prevent it from turning bitter.

PURÉE: Combine the water and salt in a large pot over high heat. Bring to boil, add the celeriac, return to boil and reduce to simmer over medium heat. Cook until tender, about 15 to 20 minutes. Drain and transfer to a food processor. Process the celeriac, add the milk and olive oil and continue to process until very smooth, about 2 minutes. Season with salt and black pepper. Keep warm.

GRILL: Combine the broth, oil, paprika, salt, black pepper, oregano, thyme, cayenne, and garlic in a shallow dish, mixing well. Add the tofu and coat well on all sides with the marinade. Set aside to marinate for 5 minutes while you preheat the grill pan.

Preheat a grill pan over medium heat, turning on the exhaust fan. Grill the tofu until marks appear, about 4 minutes per side, rotating the tofu a quarter turn after 2 minutes.

ARTICHOKES: Heat the oil in a medium skillet over medium-high heat. Add the artichokes and cook, stirring occasionally, until the artichokes are golden, about 7 minutes. Add the garlic and cook until the artichokes are crisp on some of the leaves and the garlic is golden brown.

ASSEMBLY: Serve the warm purée in bowls, topped with artichokes and 2 slices of tofu. Drizzle with a half teaspoon of olive oil, if desired.

 QUICK TIPS: Begin by pressing the tofu and heating the water. Heat the water to boil before adding the celeriac to keep the celeriac from turning bitter; peel and chop the celeriac while the water heats. Prepare the marinade while the tofu presses. Preheat the grill pan while the tofu marinates. Begin cooking the artichokes when you flip the tofu. Process the celeriac when you begin cooking the artichokes.

sambal-glazed tempeh bowl

SERVES 4 | GF, SFO

This is a beautifully fiery, spicy dish, as the name implies. The sauce is sweet and spicy, but some of the heat dissipates with the grilling. However, if you are a lover of spice, drizzle the bowl with the remainder of the sauce.

RICE

- 1 1/2 cups water
- 1/2 teaspoon salt
- 1 cup long-grain white or basmati rice

GRILL

- 6 tablespoons rice wine vinegar
- 6 tablespoons sambal oelek
- 3 tablespoons reduced-sodium tamari
- 2 tablespoons fresh lime juice
- 1 tablespoon jarred caper brine liquid
- 4 tablespoons natural sugar
- 2 teaspoons finely grated ginger
- 8 ounces tempeh, cut into 1/2-inch slices

PEPITAS

- 1/2 cup pepitas (pumpkin seeds)
- 1 teaspoon five-spice powder
- Sea salt

VEGETABLES

- 1 teaspoon toasted sesame oil
- 4 cups coarsely chopped broccoli florets
- 2 medium carrots, cut into julienne slices
- 1 cup coarsely chopped scallions, divided
- 2 tablespoons vegetable broth
- 1 tablespoon reduced-sodium tamari
- Salt and ground black pepper

SOY-FREE OPTION: Substitute 12 ounces of seitan for the tempeh. Substitute coconut aminos for the tamari, adding 1/8 teaspoon sea salt in the sambal glaze.

RICE: Heat the water and salt in a small saucepan over high heat. Rinse the rice in two changes of fresh water and add to the pan. When the water is bubbling on the sides of the pan, cover the pan, reduce the heat to low and cook for 15 minutes. Remove from the heat and set aside for 10 minutes to steam. Fluff with a fork before serving.

GRILL: Combine the vinegar, sambal oelek, tamari, lime juice, caper liquid, sugar, and ginger in a small saucepan over medium-high heat. Bring to boil and reduce to simmer over medium heat. Simmer until reduced by half, about 5 minutes, then add the tempeh and set aside. Preheat a grill pan over medium heat. Spray the pan with oil and add the tempeh. Grill, basting with the glaze often, until marks appear, about 3 minutes per side. Thin the glaze with a few tablespoons of water, if needed.

PEPITAS: Heat a large skillet over medium heat. Add the pepitas and cook for 3 minute. Stir in the 5-spice powder and season with salt. Remove from skillet and set aside.

VEGETABLES: Heat the oil in the large skillet over high heat. Add the broccoli and carrots. Stir and cook until lightly charred, about 3 minutes. Add 1/2 cup scallions. Stir and cook for 1 minute. Reduce the heat to medium, add the broth and tamari, cover and cook until the vegetables are crisp-tender, about 3 minutes. Season with salt and pepper.

ASSEMBLY: To serve, layer the rice in bowls. Top with the stir-fried vegetables, grilled tempeh and the remaining sambal sauce. Garnish with the pepitas and the remaining scallions.

QUICK TIPS: Use the same skillet for the seeds and the vegetables. Chop all the vegetables before stir-frying. Grill the tempeh and cook the vegetables at the same time.

lebanese fattoush bowl
with portobello kebabs

SERVES 4 | GFO, SF

Fattoush is a Lebanese bread salad made with pita, mint and cucumber, among other ingredients. Toum is a serious garlic sauce that pairs perfectly with the grilled mushrooms. Although traditionally toum is made with lots of oil, here I have used cashews instead, with equally delicious results.

CASHEW TOUM SAUCE

1/2 cup raw cashew pieces

1/3 cup water

1 tablespoon fresh lemon juice

2 tablespoons minced garlic

1/4 teaspoon sea salt

MUSHROOMS

1/4 cup unsweetened plain nondairy yogurt

2 tablespoons olive oil

2 tablespoons fresh lemon juice

1/2 teaspoon grated ginger

1/2 teaspoon fresh or dried thyme

1/2 teaspoon sea salt

4 small portobello mushrooms, stems and gills removed, cut into 3 pieces

8 ripe cherry tomatoes

SALAD

2 tablespoons pomegranate molasses

2 tablespoons vegetable broth

1 tablespoon olive oil

1 teaspoon sumac or 1/2 teaspoon lemon zest

3 cups coarsely chopped romaine lettuce

1/4 cup coarsely chopped mint

4 scallions, minced

1/2 medium cucumber, peeled, seeded, and cut into 1/4- inch dice

2 pita breads, toasted and cut into 2-inch pieces

Sea salt and black pepper

GLUTEN-FREE OPTION: Use thick gluten-free flatbread instead of the pita.

SAUCE: Combine the cashews with enough water to cover in a small saucepan. Cover, bring to boil, and cook for 5 minutes. Set aside for 5 minutes, drain and rinse the nuts. Transfer to a blender. Add the water, lemon juice, garlic and salt. Blend as smooth as possible.

MUSHROOMS: Combine the yogurt, oil, lemon juice, ginger, thyme, and salt in a large bowl, mixing well. Add the mushroom slices and tomatoes and toss to combine. If extra time allows, optionally skewer the middle mushroom slices and a tomato on 4 skewers. Skewer 2 mushroom ends and 1 tomato on another 4 skewers. Grill the mushrooms and tomatoes, covering the pan, until tender, about 3 minutes per side.

SALAD: Wipe out the large bowl and combine the molasses, broth, oil and sumac. Add the lettuce, mint, scallions, cucumber, and pita to the large bowl. Season with salt and pepper and toss well. Serve the mushrooms and tomatoes in shallow bowls with the fattoush and the garlic sauce.

 QUICK TIPS: To begin, heat the water for the cashews and preheat the grill pan. While the mushrooms are cooking, prepare the dressing and chop the vegetables. Skewering the mushrooms and tomatoes takes a few extra minutes.

SUBSTITUTION: Substitute 2 tablespoons of grape jelly plus either 1 1/2 teaspoons tamarind concentrate or 2 tablespoons fresh lemon juice for the pomegranate molasses. Instead of the mushrooms, use Slow-Simmered Seitan (page 11). Substitute 2 tablespoons fresh oregano for the mint.

balsamic-glazed seitan bowl
with grilled potato salad

SERVES 4 | GFO, SF

Balsamic vinegar reduces to a beautiful, sweet glaze and the acid mostly dissipates. The glaze is then cooked with the seitan and served with a lightly smoked, grilled potato salad. It's a meat-and-potatoes dish, done vegan style.

GLAZE

- 1 cup balsamic vinegar
- 1 tablespoon pure maple syrup
- 1 teaspoon olive oil
- 1 (1-inch) piece ginger, cut into 4 slices
- 2 garlic cloves
- 1 pound Slow-Simmered Seitan (page 11) or store-bought seitan, cut into 1/2-inch slices

POTATOES

- 1 pound Yukon Gold potatoes, peeled and cut into 1/2-inch thick slices
- 1 teaspoon sea salt
- 1 (1-inch) piece ginger, cut into 4 slices
- 2 garlic cloves

VEGETABLES

- 1 tablespoon olive oil
- 1/2 small green cabbage, finely shredded
- 1/2 cup raw walnut pieces
- Sea salt and black pepper

DRESSING

- 2 tablespoons olive oil
- 2 tablespoons rice vinegar
- 2 tablespoons vegetable broth
- 1 tablespoon fresh orange juice
- 1 tablespoon drained capers, minced
- 1/4 teaspoon red pepper flakes
- Sea salt and black pepper
- 2 scallions, minced

GLUTEN-FREE OPTION: Substitute 1 pound of tempeh, cut into thin triangles, for the seitan; or 4 portobello mushrooms, stemmed and gills scraped out.

GLAZE: Combine the vinegar, maple, oil, ginger, and garlic in a large pot or skillet over medium heat. Bring to a simmer and cook until reduced by half, about 6 minutes. Add the seitan and cook on low until the seitan is glazed, about 5 minutes. Remove from heat and set aside. Discard the ginger and garlic.

POTATOES: Combine the potatoes, salt, ginger, and garlic with enough water to cover in a medium saucepan over high heat. Bring to boil and reduce to simmer over medium heat. Cook until the potatoes are fork tender, about 8 minutes. Drain the potatoes. Discard the garlic and ginger, and set aside.

VEGETABLES: Heat the oil in a large skillet over medium heat. Add the cabbage, cover, and cook until softened, about 5 minutes. Stir, uncover and cook until it begins to brown. Add the walnuts and cook until golden brown, about 3 minutes. Season with salt and pepper. Remove from heat and set aside.

DRESSING: Combine the oil, vinegar, broth, and juice in a large bowl. Add the capers and red pepper flakes. Set aside.

GRILLING: Preheat a grill pan over medium heat. Grill the potatoes until crisp on the cut side and grill marks appear, about 2 minutes per side. Chop the warm potatoes, transfer them to the large bowl and season with salt and black pepper. Grill the seitan until marks appear and the seitan is hot, about 1 minute per side. To serve, tranfer the potatoes to bowls and top with the cabbage and seitan. Garnish with scallions.

 QUICK TIPS: First, heat the water for the potatoes, then prepare the glaze and then chop the potatoes. Cut the cabbage while the skillet preheats. Make the dressing while the potatoes and cabbage cook. Preheat the grill pan when the potatoes are knife-tender.

grilled summer vegetable bowl
with farro and roasted corn salad

SERVES 4 | GFO, SF

Grilling and summer are a natural match. Many fruits and vegetables are abundant at that time of year. In this salad, the grilled vegetables and the chewy farro are tossed with a bright dressing. Serve it warm or at room temperature.

FARRO

3 cups vegetable broth

1 cup pearled farro, rinsed well

2 garlic cloves

1 teaspoon dried basil

1/4 teaspoon red pepper flakes

2 cups cooked cannellini or kidney beans

1 cup corn kernels, thawed well if frozen

1/4 teaspoon mild chili powder

Sea salt and black pepper

GRILL

2 small yellow squash or zucchini, cut into 1/2-inch thick slices lengthwise

1 medium red or green bell pepper, cut into 1-inch wide pieces

1 cup ripe cherry tomatoes (about 1 pint)

6 scallions

1 teaspoon olive oil

Sea salt and black pepper

DRESSING

1/2 cup coarsely chopped cucumber

1 garlic clove, coarsely chopped

3 tablespoons olive oil

1 tablespoon fresh lemon juice

1/2 teaspoon natural sugar

1/4 teaspoon sea salt

1/2 cup minced basil

GLUTEN-FREE OPTION: Cook 1 cup of white or brown rice in the flavored broth. Cook until tender and drain. Brown rice will take about 5 to 10 more minutes to cook than farro.

FARRO: Combine the broth, farro, garlic, basil, and red pepper flakes in a medium saucepan. Bring to boil over high heat, reduce to simmer and cook until the farro is tender, about 20 minutes. Add the beans and drain. Set aside.

Heat a medium skillet over medium-high heat. Add the corn and cook, stirring occasionally, until golden brown, about 7 minutes. If using fresh corn you will need to add 1 teaspoon olive oil to the skillet. Stir in the chili powder and season with salt and black pepper. Remove from heat and set aside.

GRILL: Preheat a grill pan over medium-high heat. Toss the squash, bell pepper, tomatoes and scallions with the oil in a large bowl. Season with salt and black pepper.

Grill the squash and bell pepper until crisp-tender, about 3 minutes per side. Grill the scallions until crisp-tender, about 3 minutes. Grill the tomatoes until marks appear, about 2 minutes per side. Grill in batches to avoid overcrowding. Coarsely chop the vegetables, except the tomatoes, and transfer back to the large bowl.

DRESSING: Combine the cucumber, garlic, olive oil, lemon juice, sugar, and salt in a personal blender. Blend until smooth. Taste and adjust seasoning. Stir in the basil. Add the farro, beans, corn, and 3 to 4 tablespoons of the dressing to the vegetables. Gently toss to combine and taste and adjust seasoning. Serve in bowls with the remainder of the dressing.

 QUICK TIPS: Preheat the grill pan before you begin preparing the vegetables, as the pan will need about 5 minutes to preheat.

miso-cajun grilled sweet potato bowl

SERVES 4 | GF, SFO

The red pepper sauce is the uniting factor in this dish. You might find it tasty enough to make and add to other vegetables and grains, but in this recipe, it's a wonderful accompaniment to the grilled sweet potatoes and roasted broccoli. The miso pairs well with the Cajun flavors, as neither dominates the other.

QUINOA

- 1 cup quinoa, rinsed well
- 1 1/2 cups vegetable broth
- 1 garlic clove, crushed
- 1/4 teaspoon sea salt
- 2 cups cooked black beans

SWEET POTATOES

- 1 pound sweet potatoes, peeled and cut into 1-inch thick wedges
- 1/4 cup vegetable broth
- 2 tablespoons white miso
- 1 tablespoon olive oil
- 2 teaspoons paprika
- 1 teaspoon fresh or dried thyme
- 1 teaspoon natural sugar
- 1/2 teaspoon black pepper
- 1/2 teaspoon sea salt
- 2 garlic cloves, coarsely chopped

VEGETABLES

- 1 pound broccoli, cut into medium florets
- 1 teaspoon olive oil
- Sea salt and black pepper

SAUCE

- 1 large roasted red bell pepper, fresh or jarred
- 2 tablespoons vegetable broth
- 2 teaspoons white wine vinegar
- Sea salt and black pepper

SOY-FREE OPTION: Substitute chickpea miso for the white miso.

QUINOA: Heat the quinoa, broth, garlic, and salt in a medium saucepan. Cover, bring to boil over high heat, reduce to medium-low heat and cook, covered, for 15 minutes. Remove from heat, and set aside for 10 minutes. Fluff in the beans and keep warm.

SWEET POTATOES: Steam the potato wedges in a large pot using a steamer basket. Steam until almost tender, about 7 minutes. Preheat a grill pan over medium heat. Blend the broth, miso, oil, paprika, thyme, sugar, black pepper, salt, and garlic in a small blender. Transfer the marinade to a large bowl and coat the par-cooked sweet potatoes well, rubbing in the marinade. Grill the wedges, covered, until tender, about 2 minutes per side.

VEGETABLES: Preheat the oven to 425°F. Steam the broccoli florets in the same steamer setup until almost tender, about 4 minutes. Transfer the broccoli to a baking sheet and toss with the oil and salt and black pepper. Bake until tender and crisp on the edges, about 10 minutes.

SAUCE: Transfer the remaining marinade back to the small blender. Add the bell pepper, broth, and vinegar and season with salt and black pepper. Blend until very smooth.

ASSEMBLY: To serve, spoon the quinoa and beans in wide bowls topped with wedges of sweet potato and roasted broccoli. Serve with the sauce.

QUICK TIPS: First, heat the broth for the quinoa and the water for the steaming, then preheat the oven and preheat the grill pan. First steam the sweet potatoes, then the broccoli.

tempeh bowl with fennel sofrito
and sweet potato mofongo

* SERVES 4 | GF, SFO

Mofongo is an African-Puerto Rican dish of deep-fried starchy vegetables mashed with garlic and oil. Typically the vegetable is green plantain or cassava root. This is a more accessible recipe, since it uses starchy russet potatoes and sweet potatoes. I've also grilled the potatoes instead of frying them, and I serve them with braised fennel and tempeh. See photo on page 82.

GARLIC OIL

4 tablespoons sunflower oil

20 garlic cloves, coarsely chopped

1 teaspoon achiote (annatto) seeds

1/2 teaspoon cumin seeds

1/2 teaspoon dried oregano

1/4 teaspoon coriander seeds

1/4 teaspoon sea salt

SOFRITO

1 large onion, cut into 1/4-inch slices

8 ounces tempeh, cut into 1/2-inch thick slices

2 medium fennel bulbs, cut into 1/8-inch slices (10 to 12 ounces each)

1/4 cup dry white wine or dry vermouth

2 cups vegetable broth

1 cup cooked white beans

1/2 teaspoon sea salt

Black pepper, to taste

MOFONGO

12 ounces russet potatoes, peeled and cut into 1/2-inch thick slices

2 teaspoons olive oil, divided

12 ounces sweet potatoes, peeled and cut into 1/2-inch thick slices

Sea salt and black pepper

SOY-FREE OPTION: Omit the tempeh. Add 1 cup cooked kidney beans when adding the cannellini beans.

GARLIC OIL: Heat the oil in a small saucepan over medium heat. Add the garlic and achiote seeds and cook until golden, about 4 minutes, stirring occasionally. Add the cumin, oregano, and coriander. Cook for 30 seconds and remove from the heat. When cool enough to handle, process the mixture with the salt until smooth as possible using a blender. Set aside.

SOFRITO: Heat 1 tablespoon of the garlic oil in a large pot over medium-high heat. Add the onion and tempeh, cover and cook until golden, about 4 minutes, stirring occasionally. Add the fennel and wine and cook until evaporated. Add the broth, beans, salt, pepper and another tablespoon of the garlic oil. Simmer until the fennel is tender and the sauce almost completely reduces, about 12 minutes.

MOFONGO: Preheat a grill pan over medium heat. Toss the russet potato slices with 1 teaspoon oil and grill until tender, about 4 minute per side, covering the pan. Toss the sweet potatoes with the remaining 1 teaspoon oil and grill until tender, about 2 minutes per side, covered. If the potatoes are not tender, add them to the pan directly on top of the sweet potatoes during the last 2 minutes of grilling. Mash the potatoes with 2 tablespoons of the garlic oil and season to taste with salt and pepper. Set aside but keep warm. Serve the mofongo with the sofrito and a side of the garlic oil for dipping.

QUICK TIPS: Preheat the oil while you chop the garlic. Chop the onion and the fennel while the oil cools. Peel and chop the russets while the grill pan preheats. Peel and chop the sweet potatoes while the russets grill.

vegan chef's salad bowl (page 119)

seven | salad bowls

Salads, especially raw leafy greens, provide essential nutrients that help maintain our healthy vegan diets. The easiest way to incorporate raw leafy greens into our diet is by eating large, meal-size salads. To maximize nutrients and keep salads from getting boring, these recipes combine raw greens with a variety of different plant proteins and other ingredients. Not only are these recipes unique, but they expand the notion of a typical salad. The BLT Club Salad transforms black beans into a smoky, salty delight, with croutons and a creamy ranch-style dressing. The Tapenade Panzanella turns the traditionally day-old bread into olive-baked croutons. The salad is then enhanced with a variety of raw and sautéed vegetables and topped with an easy vinaigrette. Lesson learned: think outside the salad bowl!

spinach salad bowl
with warm pecan dressing

SERVES 4 | GF, SF

This is a spin on spinach salad with warm bacon dressing. This salad is filled with shaved fennel, perfectly cooked quinoa, and candied pecans. The warm orange-pecan dressing ties all the flavors together and delivers a delicious, filling salad.

QUINOA

1 cup quinoa, rinsed well

1 1/2 cups vegetable broth

1 garlic clove, crushed

1/4 teaspoon sea salt

DRESSING

1 cup raw pecan pieces

5 tablespoons fresh orange juice, divided

2 teaspoons pure maple syrup, divided

3 tablespoons grapeseed oil

1 tablespoon plus 1 teaspoon white wine vinegar

1 tablespoon vegetable broth

SALAD

8 cups coarsely chopped fresh spinach (about 2 bunches, tough stems removed)

1 cup shaved fennel (about 1 small bulb)

QUINOA: Combine the quinoa, broth, garlic, and salt in a small saucepan. Cover, bring to boil over high heat, reduce to medium-low heat, and cook for 15 minutes. Remove from heat and set aside for 10 minutes. Fluff with a fork before serving.

DRESSING: Toast the nuts in a small skillet over medium heat, stirring frequently, until golden, about 4 minutes. Remove from heat and transfer half of the nuts to a small blender. Add 2 tablespoons juice and 1 teaspoon maple syrup to the nuts in the skillet. Cook until the liquid evaporates, about 3 minutes. Transfer the glazed nuts to a parchment paper and set aside to cool.

Add the remaining 3 tablespoons of juice, 1 teaspoon maple syrup, oil, vinegar, and broth to the blender. Blend until smooth. Season with salt and black pepper. When ready to serve, warm the dressing in the small skillet and add about half of the warm dressing to a large bowl.

SALAD: Add the spinach and fennel and toss. To serve, divide the salad and quinoa among wide bowls and serve with the remaining dressing. Alternatively, toss the salad with the quinoa and serve with the remaining dressing.

QUICK TIPS: While you rinse the quinoa, heat the broth. Juice the orange while the nuts toast. Prepare the juice near the stove to keep an eye on the nuts. To shave fennel, cut off the top, cut in half, then slice into very thin slices, preferably using a mandoline.

two-bean salad bowl
with pesto dressing

SERVES 4 | GF, SF

Green beans and chickpeas come together in this hearty salad. The green beans are tossed in a flavorful pesto and the chickpeas are roasted with almonds and a salty and spicy rub. Quinoa adds plenty of protein and the salad greens bring a freshness to the plate.

QUINOA

- 1 cup quinoa, well rinsed
- 1 1/2 cups vegetable broth
- 1/4 teaspoon sea salt

PESTO

- 6 tablespoons vegetable broth
- 3 tablespoons tahini
- 2 tablespoons fresh lemon juice
- 2 ounces basil, leaves only
- 1 garlic clove
- 1/4 teaspoon sea salt
- Black pepper, to taste

BEANS

- 1 pound green beans, trimmed, cut into thirds
- 1 teaspoon olive oil
- 2 cups cooked chickpeas
- 1 teaspoon fresh or dried thyme
- 1/2 cup whole raw almonds
- 1/2 teaspoon sea salt
- 1/2 teaspoon paprika
- 1/8 to 1/4 teaspoon cayenne

SALAD

- 3 cups coarsely chopped romaine lettuce
- 1 cup grape or cherry tomatoes, halved
- 1/4 cup sliced red onion, cut into paper-thin slices

QUINOA: Combine the quinoa, broth, and salt in a small saucepan. Cover, bring to boil over high heat, reduce to medium-low heat, and cook for 15 minutes. Remove from heat and set aside for 10 minutes. Fluff with a fork before serving.

PESTO: Combine the broth, tahini, lemon juice, basil, garlic, salt and pepper in a blender. Blend until smooth. Taste and adjust seasoning. Set aside.

BEANS: Steam the green beans until tender, 4 to 5 minutes, using a steamer basket set in a large pot. Transfer to a bowl, toss with 1/3 of the pesto, and set aside.

Heat the oil in a large skillet over medium-high heat. Add the chickpeas and thyme. Cook, stirring occasionally, until they begin to brown, about 3 minutes. Add the almonds and continue to cook until golden, about 3 more minutes. Remove from heat and stir in the salt, paprika, and cayenne.

SALAD: Combine the romaine, tomatoes, and onion with 2 tablespoons of pesto in a large bowl and toss to mix. Divide the salad, quinoa, green beans, and chickpea mixture among four bowls, keeping the ingredients relatively separate so diners can combine them as they desire. Serve with the remaining pesto.

QUICK TIPS: Rinse the quinoa while the broth heats. Prepare the steamer basket with water and bring to a simmer. Chop the lettuce, tomatoes, and onion while the chickpeas are cooking.

hearts of palm and quinoa bowl
with citrus-oregano vinaigrette

SERVES 4 | GF, SFO

The Citrus-Oregano Vinaigrette is purposely acidic. The sweetness of the candied pecans balances the acidity of the dressing, and the roasted garlic adds its own sweetness. If you can't find hearts of palm, use 1 (14-ounce) can of artichoke hearts, quartered.

QUINOA
- 1 cup quinoa, rinsed well
- 1 1/2 cups vegetable broth
- 1 garlic clove, crushed
- 1/4 teaspoon sea salt

PECANS
- 1 cup raw pecan pieces
- 3 tablespoons maple syrup
- 1 1/2 tablespoons reduced-sodium tamari

DRESSING
- 1/4 cup fresh lemon juice
- 3 tablespoons olive oil
- 1 tablespoon water
- 2 tablespoons fresh oregano (do not use dried)
- Sea salt and black pepper, to taste

SALAD
- 6 cups coarsely chopped romaine lettuce
- 2 cups arugula, coarsely chopped if desired
- 1 large carrot, shredded or cut into julienne slices
- 1 cup shredded purple cabbage
- 2 teaspoons olive oil
- 6 garlic cloves, cut into 1/8-inch slices
- 1 (14-ounce) can whole hearts of palm, drained, rinsed, and cut into 1-inch medallions

SOY-FREE OPTION: Substitute coconut aminos with 1/8 teaspoon sea salt for the tamari.

QUINOA: Combine the quinoa, broth, garlic and salt in a small saucepan. Cover, bring to boil over high heat, reduce to medium-low heat and cook for 15 minutes. Remove from heat and set aside for 10 minutes. Fluff with a fork before serving.

PECANS: Combine the pecans, maple syrup, and tamari in a medium saucepan. Heat over medium heat and cook until the syrup reduces and becomes sticky, stirring frequently, 4 to 5 minutes. Transfer to a parchment paper and cool.

DRESSING: Combine the juice, oil, water, and oregano in a small blender. Blend until as smooth as possible. Add salt and pepper, to taste.

SALAD: Combine the lettuce, arugula, carrot, cabbage, pecans, and quinoa with half the dressing in a large bowl. Toss well and divide the salad among 4 bowls. Heat the oil in a large skillet over medium heat. Add the garlic and cook until light golden brown, about 1 minute. Remove the garlic slices and add to the salad. Add the hearts of palm, cut-side down, to the skillet and cook until golden, about 2 minutes per side. Season with salt and black pepper. To serve, divide the hearts of palm among the four bowls. Alternatively, add the hearts of palm to the salad ingredients in the large bowl before serving. Serve with the remaining dressing.

QUICK TIPS: Heat the vegetable broth while rinsing the quinoa. Remember to set the timer for the quinoa. Chop some of the vegetables near the stove while the nuts and quinoa are cooking. Use a mandoline or julienne peeler to cut the carrots. Rinse the hearts of palm using the strainer.

buffalo chickpea salad bowl

SERVES 4 | GFO, SF

Ever since Buffalo wings were popularized by a small bar in New York City, it seems everything, even in the vegan culinary world, has been tossed in the cayenne-based sauce. After thirty years of popularity, it seems the Buffalo sauce is here to stay. This salad combines chickpeas with the spicy sauce and mellows the flavors with a cooling avocado dressing.

DRESSING

- 1/4 cup raw cashew pieces
- 1/4 cup vegetable broth
- 1/2 ripe Hass avocado, peeled and pitted
- 1/4 cup parsley
- 1 tablespoon fresh lime juice
- Sea salt and black pepper, to taste

BEANS

- 1 teaspoon olive oil
- 2 cups cooked chickpeas
- 1 garlic clove, minced
- 1/2 cup Louisiana-style hot sauce
- 1/4 cup vegetable broth
- Sea salt and black pepper, to taste

CROUTONS

- 2 tablespoons grapeseed oil
- 4 cups cubed day-old bread
- 1 teaspoon dried thyme
- 1/2 teaspoon garlic powder
- Sea salt and black pepper
- 1 teaspoon smoked paprika

SALAD

- 8 cups coarsely chopped romaine lettuce
- 2 medium carrots, cut into julienne strips
- 2 celery ribs, cut into 1/8-inch slices on a diagonal

GLUTEN-FREE OPTION: Use gluten-free bread for the croutons.

DRESSING: Combine the cashews and enough water to cover in a small saucepan. Cover, bring to a boil, and cook for 5 minutes. Remove from the heat and set aside for 5 minutes. Drain, rinse with cool water, and transfer to a small blender. Add the broth, avocado, parsley, lime juice, salt, and pepper. Blend until smooth and set aside.

BEANS: Heat the oil in a large skillet over medium-high heat. Add the chickpeas and cook until golden, about 5 minutes. Add the garlic and cook for 30 seconds. Add the hot sauce and broth. Cook until the liquid evaporates, 5 to 8 minutes. Transfer to a small bowl, season with salt and pepper, and set aside to cool.

CROUTONS: Wipe out the skillet with a damp cloth. Heat the oil in the skillet over medium heat. Stir in the bread and cook until golden brown, about 4 minutes. Stir in the thyme and garlic powder and season with salt and black pepper. Stir and cook until the bread is crunchy, about 5 more minutes. Stir in the paprika and set aside.

SALAD: Combine the lettuce, carrots, celery, and 2 tablespoons dressing in a large bowl. Toss to combine. Transfer the salad to four bowls. Divide the beans and croutons among the bowls. Add more dressing as desired. Serve.

 QUICK TIPS: Begin by heating the water for the cashews. Prepare the lettuce, carrots, and celery while the beans and croutons are cooking. Use a mandoline or julienne peeler to cut the carrots. Chop near the stove so you can easily keep an eye on the chickpeas.

tapenade panzanella bowl

SERVES 4 | SF

This salad is unlike any panzanella you've ever had before, mostly because there is nothing like the croutons in this salad: Kalamata olives are minced extra-fine before being added to the crouton marinade. The bread is tossed with the marinade and then baked to golden deliciousness.

BREAD

- 6 tablespoons vegetable broth
- 3 tablespoons fresh lemon juice, preferably Meyer lemon
- 2 tablespoons olive oil
- 4 garlic cloves, coarsely chopped
- 2 teaspoons Dijon mustard
- Black pepper
- 1/4 cup pitted and finely minced kalamata olives
- 8 ounces day-old artisan bread, torn into bite-size pieces

VEGETABLES

- 1 small summer squash, cut into 1/2-inch slices lengthwise
- 1 teaspoon olive oil, for grilling
- 1 teaspoon maple syrup
- 2 cups ripe cherry tomatoes, halved
- 2 cups coarsely chopped lettuce
- 1/2 cup coarsely chopped roasted red bell peppers
- 2 scallions, finely chopped
- 1/2 large cucumber, peeled, seeded, and coarsely chopped
- 1 cup cooked black beans
- 1/4 cup pitted oil-cured black olives (optional)
- Sea salt and black pepper, to taste

BREAD: Preheat the oven to 375°F. Combine the vegetable broth, lemon juice, oil, garlic, mustard, and black pepper, to taste, in a small blender and blend until smooth. Transfer 1/4 cup of the dressing to a large bowl and stir in the minced kalamata olives. Add the bread pieces and toss to combine. Transfer to a baking sheet. Bake the bread until crisp, about 15 minutes, turning the pieces after 10 minutes. Set aside.

VEGETABLES: Heat a grill pan over medium heat. Brush the squash slices with the olive oil. Grill the slices until tender, about 4 minutes per side. When the squash is cool enough to handle, chop into bite-size pieces.

ASSEMBLY: Combine the remaining dressing, maple syrup, crisp bread, grilled squash, tomatoes, lettuce, bell pepper, scallions, cucumber, beans, and olives (if using) in a large bowl. Toss to combine. Season with salt and pepper. Divide among four bowls and serve.

QUICK TIPS: Preheat the grill pan before preparing the squash, as the pan will need about 5 minutes to preheat. Chop the tomatoes, cucumbers, and lettuce while the squash is grilling. Chop near the stove so you can easily keep an eye on the squash. Don't forget to set your timer for the oven.

greek quinoa salad bowl
with pickled onions

SERVES 4 | GF, SFO

This is a favorite of ours, and we love it served with a creamy vegan cheese or a chopped ripe avocado. The dressing is wonderfully creamy and is truly best made with vegan mayo. However, if you are looking for a healthier option, substitute unsweetened plain vegan soy yogurt.

QUINOA
- 1 cup quinoa, rinsed well
- 1 1/2 cups vegetable broth
- 1 garlic clove, crushed
- 1/4 teaspoon sea salt

PICKLED ONIONS
- 3 tablespoons white wine vinegar
- 2 tablespoons water
- 1 tablespoon olive oil
- 1 teaspoon lemon juice
- 1 garlic clove, minced
- 1 teaspoon dried oregano
- 1 teaspoon natural sugar
- 1/4 teaspoon sea salt
- Black pepper, to taste
- 1/2 medium red onion, cut into paper-thin slices

DRESSING
- 1 tablespoon olive oil
- 1/4 cup vegan mayo

VEGETABLES
- 2 cups baby kale or baby spinach
- 2 cups coarsely chopped romaine lettuce
- 2 cups cooked black beans
- 1 medium roasted red pepper, freshly roasted or jarred, chopped
- 1 medium carrot, shredded
- 1 medium tomato, seeded and coarsely chopped
- 1/2 cup pitted and chopped kalamata olives
- 1 ripe Hass avocado, pitted, peeled and diced

SOY-FREE OPTION: Use a soy-free mayonnaise.

QUINOA: Combine the quinoa, broth, garlic, and salt in a small saucepan. Cover, bring to boil over high heat, reduce to medium-low heat and cook for 15 minutes. Remove from heat and set aside for 10 minutes. Fluff with a fork before serving.

PICKLED ONIONS: Combine the vinegar, water, oil, lemon juice, garlic, oregano, sugar, salt, and black pepper in a medium bowl. Add the onion and mix well. Set aside for 20 minutes.

DRESSING: Drain off 2 tablespoons of this brine and transfer it to a small bowl. Stir in the oil and mix well with a whisk. Stir in the mayo and mix well. Taste and adjust seasoning, adding another tablespoon of brine, if desired.

VEGETABLES: Combine the kale, romaine, beans, red pepper, carrot, tomato, and olives in a large bowl. Serve the salad in bowls, quinoa to the side, pickled onions and avocado on top, and drizzled with the dressing. Alternatively, toss the salad with the quinoa and dressing and serve topped with the onions and avocado.

QUICK TIPS: Begin by heating the broth for the quinoa. Chop the avocado right before serving to avoid discoloration.

chicken-free goi ga bowl

SERVES 4 | GF, SFO

Goi ga is an herbaceous Vietnamese chicken salad with a light, tart dressing. It is fresh and full of flavor. This salad is all of the above as well as quickly made and healthy, using tempeh that is simmered with ginger and garlic.

TEMPEH

1 tablespoon grapeseed oil

3 cloves garlic, minced

1 (1-inch) piece ginger, grated

8 ounces tempeh, cut into 1-inch pieces

1 cup vegetable broth

DRESSING

3 tablespoons seasoned rice vinegar

1 tablespoon reduced-sodium tamari

1 tablespoon fresh lime juice

2 teaspoons jarred caper brine liquid

1 teaspoon water

1 teaspoon sambal oelek

1 tablespoon natural sugar

1/8 teaspoon sea salt

1 tablespoon seeded and thinly sliced jalapeño

SALAD

5 cups coarsely chopped napa cabbage (about 12 ounces)

2 medium carrots, cut into julienne strips

4 scallions, minced

2 red radishes, cut into paper-thin slices

1/2 cup finely chopped mint leaves

1/2 cup finely chopped cilantro

1/2 cup chopped roasted peanuts

Sea salt and black pepper, to taste

SOY-FREE OPTION: Substitute 8 ounces of seitan cut into 1/2-inch cubes or 2 cups of cauliflower florets. Cook the cauliflower until tender. Substitute coconut aminos with a few pinches of sea salt for the tamari.

SUBSTITUTION: Substitute 4 cups finely chopped green cabbage for the napa cabbage.

TEMPEH: Heat the oil in a medium saucepan over medium heat. Add the garlic and ginger and cook for 30 seconds until fragrant. Add the tempeh and cook until golden brown, about 4 minutes, stirring frequently. Add the broth and simmer until the liquid is almost evaporated, about 10 minutes. Drain off any remaining broth and set tempeh aside to cool slightly.

DRESSING: Combine the vinegar, tamari, lime juice, caper liquid, water, sambal oelek, sugar, salt, and jalapeño in a small bowl. Mix well until the sugar dissolves, and add the dressing to the drained, warm tempeh in the saucepan. Toss to combine.

SALAD: Combine the cabbage, carrot, scallions, radishes, mint, cilantro, and peanuts in a large bowl. Add the tempeh and dressing. Toss to combine. Season with salt and pepper and serve in bowls.

 QUICK TIPS: Prepare the vegetables while the tempeh is simmering and marinating. Use a mandoline or julienne peeler to cut the carrots.

blt club salad with quick croutons

SERVES 4 | GFO, SFO

A sandwich made into a salad! This is a quick salad to throw together that emulates what a great vegan BLT is all about. The beans are smoky, the dressing is optionally creamy, and the croutons are the perfect finishing touch.

BEANS

1 teaspoon grapeseed oil

1 garlic clove, minced

2 cups cooked black beans, patted dry

1 tablespoon reduced-sodium tamari

1 teaspoon smoked paprika

CROUTONS

2 tablespoons grapeseed oil

4 cups cubed day-old bread

1 teaspoon dried thyme

1/2 teaspoon garlic powder

Sea salt and black pepper

1 teaspoon smoked paprika

SALAD

1/4 cup vegan mayonnaise or 2 tablespoons
    grapeseed oil

2 tablespoons seasoned rice vinegar

6 cups shredded lettuce

1 cup sliced grape or cherry tomatoes

1 cup alfalfa sprouts

1 small ripe Hass avocado, pitted, peeled, and
    coarsely chopped (optional)

GLUTEN-FREE OPTION: Use gluten-free bread for the croutons.

SOY-FREE OPTION: Substitute coconut aminos with a few pinches of sea salt for the tamari.

BEANS: Heat the oil in a medium saucepan over medium heat. Stir in the garlic and beans and cook 2 minutes until heated. Stir in the tamari and paprika. Cook until the liquid evaporates. Set aside to cool.

CROUTONS: Heat the oil in a large skillet over medium heat. Stir in the bread and cook until golden brown, about 4 minutes. Stir in the thyme and garlic powder and season with salt and black pepper. Stir and cook until the bread is crunchy, about 5 more minutes. Stir in the paprika and set aside.

SALAD: Combine the mayo or oil and vinegar in a large bowl using a whisk. Add the lettuce, tomatoes, sprouts, avocado (if using), and reserved beans and toss gently. Season to taste with salt and black pepper. Top with the croutons and serve immediately.

QUICK TIPS: Chop the lettuce and tomatoes while the croutons are cooking. Chop near the stove so you can easily stir the bread.

vegan chef's salad bowl

SERVES 4

Chef's salads are typically laden with lunch meats, cheeses, and egg. This vegan version features protein from lentils and tofu, and is accompanied by a bold dressing that is capable of standing up to the other hearty ingredients. The croutons from page 111 make a crunchy addition to this recipe. (See photo on page 104.)

LENTILS

2 1/2 cups vegetable broth

2 tablespoons reduced-sodium tamari

2 garlic cloves, crushed

1 cup black or green lentils, picked over and rinsed

1 tablespoon smoked paprika

2 bay leaves

1/2 teaspoon toasted sesame oil

Black pepper

TOFU

1 teaspoon grapeseed oil

1 (14-ounce) package firm or extra-firm tofu, rinsed
and squeezed of liquid, mashed

1 garlic clove, minced

1 teaspoon dried oregano

1/4 teaspoon sea salt

1/4 teaspoon ground turmeric

1/4 cup vegetable broth

DRESSING

4 tablespoons white wine vinegar

3 tablespoons grapeseed oil

2 tablespoons water

2 teaspoons Dijon mustard

2 soft sun-dried tomatoes, coarsely chopped

1 teaspoon fresh or 1/2 teaspoon dried thyme

VEGETABLES

4 cups coarsely chopped romaine lettuce

4 cups arugula, coarsely chopped if desired

1/4 cup thin sliced red onion

1 cup cherry tomatoes, halved

1 small cucumber, cut into half-moon slices

1 ripe Hass avocado, pitted, peeled, and diced

Croutons, store-bought or homemade (page 111)

LENTILS: Combine the broth, tamari, garlic, lentils, paprika, and bay leaves in a medium saucepan. Cover, bring to boil over high heat, reduce to simmer over medium heat, partially cover and cook until just tender, about 20 minutes. Drain, remove and discard the bay leaves, return the lentils to the pan and stir in the oil and pepper, to taste.

TOFU: Heat the oil in a large skillet over medium-high heat. Add the mashed tofu, garlic, oregano, salt, and turmeric. Stir and cook until lightly golden brown, about 5 minutes. Add the broth, cover and cook until the broth evaporates, about 2 minutes. Taste and adjust seasoning.

DRESSING: Combine the vinegar, oil, water, mustard, tomatoes and thyme in a small blender. Blend until smooth. Taste and adjust seasoning.

VEGETABLES: Combine the lettuce and arugula in a large bowl with a third of the dressing. Toss well. Serve the greens in bowls with the toppings layered on the greens side-by-side, including the onion, cherry tomatoes, cucumber, avocado, lentils, and tofu. Top with croutons and serve with the remaining dressing.

 QUICK TIPS: Preheat the large skillet before you press the tofu. Prepare all the garlic at the same time: 2 crushed, 2 minced. To press the tofu, squeeze half the tofu with your hands over the sink until most of the liquid is squeezed out. Repeat with the other half. Use your hands to mash the tofu. Make the dressing while the tofu cooks. Chop the vegetables while the lentils cook. Chop the avocado right before serving to prevent discoloration.

acorn squash salad bowl
with horseradish dressing

SERVES 4 | GFO, SF

Dill is such a welcoming herb, one that is especially wonderful in the middle of autumn, as it is fresh and light. Adding lemon juice to the dressing enhances the citrus notes of the dill, and the salad is served with seasonal cabbage and apple—another natural flavor match. Tossing the baked acorn squash with the dressing enriches the flavors of the sweet winter squash.

SQUASH

- 1 medium acorn squash, halved and seeded
- 1/2 cup water

FREEKEH

- 2 1/2 cups vegetable broth
- 1 cup cracked freekeh
- 1/4 cup dried apples, coarsely chopped
- 1/2 teaspoon sea salt

DRESSING

- 2 tablespoons minced dill weed
- 3 tablespoons grapeseed oil
- 2 tablespoons prepared horseradish
- 2 tablespoons fresh lemon juice
- 1 tablespoon water
- Pinch sugar
- Sea salt and black pepper, to taste

SALAD

- 3 cups finely shredded green cabbage
- 1 small apple, any kind, cut into julienne slices
- 1/4 cup minced dill weed

GLUTEN-FREE OPTION: Substitute quinoa, well rinsed, for the freekeh. Reduce the broth to 1 3/4 cups. Combine the quinoa, broth, apples and salt in a small saucepan. Cover, bring to boil over high heat, reduce to medium-low heat and cook for 15 minutes. Remove from heat and set aside for 10 minutes. Fluff with a fork before serving.

SQUASH: Preheat oven to 450°F. Place the squash, cut side down, on a baking sheet. Add the water to the sheet and bake until the squash is tender, about 20 minutes. Using a spoon or an ice cream scooper, remove the squash from the shell and transfer to a medium bowl. Set aside.

FREEKEH: Combine the broth, freekeh, dried apples and salt in a medium saucepan over medium-high heat. Bring to boil, reduce to simmer and cook until the freekeh is tender, about 15 to 20 minutes. Drain if necessary and set aside.

DRESSING: Combine the dill, oil, horseradish, lemon juice, water, sugar, salt, and pepper in a small bowl. Whisk to combine and taste and adjust seasoning. Add half of the dressing to the squash while it is still warm.

SALAD: Combine the cabbage, apple, and dill in large bowl. Add as much of the dressing as needed, without over-dressing the salad. Serve the salad in bowls, topped with the freekeh and the roasted squash.

 QUICK TIPS: Begin by preheating the oven to 450°F, then heat the broth for the freekeh. Use an ice cream scoop to seed the squash.

hungarian seitan salad bowl

SERVES 4 | GFO, SF

This is a unique salad in the sense that Hungarians do not have a great selection of traditional salad recipes. Odd for a country that mostly subsisted on vegetarian meals throughout its history. The only certain thing is that Hungarians love their salads with plenty of acid to cut through richness. This salad is very much a "meat-and-potatoes" dish and benefits greatly from the acidic dressing. For a gluten-free version, substitute diced extra-firm tofu for the seitan and cornstarch for the flour.

DRESSING

- 2 teaspoons grapeseed oil
- 1 medium onion, finely chopped
- 5 tablespoons cold water
- 3 tablespoons white wine vinegar
- 1 garlic clove
- 1 teaspoon dry mustard
- Sea salt and black pepper, to taste
- 1 teaspoon natural sugar (optional)

POTATOES

- 2 medium potatoes, any kind, peeled and cut into 1-inch cubes
- 1/2 teaspoon sea salt

SEITAN

- 2 tablespoons grapeseed oil
- 1 teaspoon toasted sesame oil
- 4 garlic cloves, finely minced
- 1 tablespoon Hungarian paprika
- 1/2 teaspoon sea salt
- 1 pound Slow-Simmered Seitan (page 11) or store-bought, cut into 1/4-inch thick strips
- 1/4 cup whole-wheat pastry or all-purpose flour
- Sea salt and black pepper, to taste

SALAD

- 6 cups coarsely chopped romaine lettuce
- 2 cups shredded red cabbage or 2 medium carrots, shredded
- 1 ripe medium tomato, coarsely chopped or 1 cup grape tomatoes
- 1 small green bell pepper, cut into julienne strips
- 1/2 medium cucumber, cut into half-moons

DRESSING: Heat the oil in a large skillet over medium heat. Add the onion, cover the skillet and cook, stirring occasionally, until caramelized, about 8 minutes. Transfer the onion to a blender, add the water, vinegar, garlic, and mustard. Blend until smooth. Taste and season with salt, pepper, and sugar, if using. Blend again and set aside.

POTATOES: Combine the potatoes, salt, and enough water to cover in a medium saucepan over high heat, covered. Bring to boil, reduce to simmer, uncover and cook until fork-tender, about 15 minutes. Drain and toss with 2 tablespoon of the dressing. Set aside.

SEITAN: Combine the oils, garlic, paprika, salt, and seitan in a medium bowl. Using your hands, massage the spices into the seitan. Sprinkle with the flour and toss again. Heat the same large skillet over medium-high heat. Add the seitan and cook until golden brown, stirring as needed to keep the seitan from burning, about 4 minutes, in batches if needed. Season with salt and pepper.

SALAD: Combine the lettuce, cabbage, tomato, bell pepper and cucumber with the remaining dressing in a large bowl and toss to coat. Divide the salad, potatoes, and seitan among four bowls. Serve.

 QUICK TIPS: First, preheat the skillet and pot of water (for the potatoes). Prepare the potatoes while the water is heating. Prepare the seitan and salad ingredients while the potatoes are cooking. Continue chopping vegetables while the seitan cooks, cutting near the stove to keep an eye on the seitan.

pad prik king tofu salad bowl

SERVES 4 | GF, SFO

Hands down, this is our favorite dish to order at Thai restaurants. It is as spicy as you make it, depending on the heat level of the red curry paste. Use as much or as little as you like, but be aware that the salad itself offers a welcome reprieve from the spice, so chances are good that you can make it a bit hotter than you may think is wise.

RICE

- 1 1/2 cups water
- 1 teaspoon sea salt
- 1 cups long-grain white rice

CURRY

- 1 (14-ounce) package firm or extra-firm tofu, pressed 5 to 10 minutes
- 1 tablespoon grapeseed oil
- 1/2 cup Red Pepper Curry Paste (page 14) or 2 to 4 tablespoons store-bought (to taste)
- 8 ounces green beans, trimmed and cut into thirds
- 1 medium red bell pepper, cut into 1/4-inch strips
- 1/2 cup water
- 2 tablespoons reduced-sodium tamari
- 1 tablespoon natural sugar
- 5 (2-lobed) kaffir lime leaves or 1 tablespoon lime zest
- Sea salt to taste

SALAD

- 4 cups finely shredded cabbage
- 1 teaspoon fresh lime juice
- 1 teaspoon toasted sesame oil

SOY-FREE OPTION: Substitute 1 small head cauliflower, cut into bite-size florets, for the tofu. Steam the florets until tender. Add the cauliflower to the skillet as you would add the fried tofu. Substitute coconut aminos with 1/8 teaspoon sea salt for the tamari.

SUBSTITUTION: Substitute 30-Minute Brown Rice (page 16) for the white rice if you have a few additional minutes.

RICE: Heat the water and salt in a small saucepan over high heat. Rinse the rice in two changes of fresh water and add to the pan. When the water is bubbling on the sides of the pan, cover the pan, reduce the heat to low and cook for 15 minutes. Remove from the heat and set aside for 10 minutes to steam. Fluff with a fork before serving.

CURRY: Cut the tofu in half lengthwise and cut the halves into 1/2-inch-thick squares. Heat the oil in a large skillet over medium-high heat. Cook the tofu until golden brown, about 3 minutes per side, in batches if needed. Remove the tofu and set aside. Add the curry paste and cook for 1 minute, stirring as needed. Add the green beans and bell peppers and cook, stirring, for 4 minutes until the beans are crisp-tender. Add the reserved tofu, water, tamari, sugar, and lime leaves. Stir to combine and cook until the sauce reduces by half, about 1 minute. Taste and season with salt. Remove and discard lime leaves.

SALAD: Combine the cabbage, lime juice, and oil in a large bowl, tossing to mix. Season with salt. Divide the salad, rice, and tofu mixture among four bowls. Serve.

QUICK TIPS: Begin by pressing the tofu. Preheat the skillet before cutting the tofu. Cut the green beans and bell pepper while the tofu cooks. Chop the cabbage while the green beans cook. Prep near the stove so you can watch the skillet.

sizzling southwestern fajita salad bowl

SERVES 4 | GF, SF

I love fajitas, and it is usually the only thing I order when I'm dining in a Mexican restaurant. Unfortunately, the vegetables offered in many restaurant fajitas are often little more than a few pieces of squash and mushroom. My fajita salad bowl is packed with colorful vegetables and even includes smoky, spicy lentils.

LENTILS

- 2 1/2 cups vegetable broth
- 1 cup black or green lentils, picked over and rinsed
- 2 garlic cloves, crushed
- 2 teaspoons dried oregano
- 2 teaspoons cumin seeds
- 1 teaspoon Chipotle Purée (page 14)
- Sea salt and black pepper, to taste

VEGETABLES

- 2 tablespoons vegetable broth
- 1 teaspoon grapeseed oil
- 3 garlic cloves, minced
- 2 teaspoons chili powder
- 2 teaspoons paprika
- 1/2 teaspoon sea salt
- Black pepper, to taste
- 2 small zucchini or summer squash, cut lengthwise into 1/2-inch slices
- 1 small red bell pepper, cut into 2-inch slices
- 1 small sweet potato, peeled and cut lengthwise into 1/4-inch slices

DRESSING

- 3 tablespoons grapeseed oil
- 3 tablespoons vegetable broth
- 2 tablespoons fresh lime juice
- 2 scallions, coarsely chopped
- 1 garlic clove, coarsely chopped
- 1 teaspoon natural sugar
- Sea salt and black pepper, to taste

SALAD

- 6 cups coarsely chopped romaine lettuce
- 1 ripe Hass avocado, pitted, peeled, and cut into 1/4-inch slices
- 1/2 cup ripe grape or cherry tomatoes, halved
- 2 cups tortilla chips, broken
- Cilantro leaves (optional)

LENTILS: Combine the broth, lentils, garlic, oregano, and cumin in a medium saucepan. Cover, bring to boil over high heat, reduce to simmer over medium heat, partially cover and cook until just tender, about 20 minutes. Drain, return to the pan, and stir in the chipotle and salt and black pepper, to taste.

VEGETABLES: Combine the broth, oil, garlic, chili powder, paprika, salt, and pepper in a large bowl. Add the zucchini, bell pepper and potato. Toss well. Cook the vegetables in batches in a lightly oiled large skillet, covered, over medium-high heat, until tender, 3 to 4 minutes per side for the potato and 2 to 3 minutes for the other vegetables. Cook in batches, transfer to a work surface and coarsely chop.

DRESSING: Combine the oil, broth, lime juice, scallions, garlic, sugar, salt, and pepper in a small blender. Blend until smooth. Taste and adjust seasoning.

ASSEMBLY: Toss the lettuce with 2 to 3 tablespoons of the dressing in a large bowl. Divide the lettuce, avocado, tomato, vegetables, lentils, tortilla chips, and cilantro, if using, among four bowls. Serve with the remaining dressing.

QUICK TIPS: Prepare the vegetables while the lentils cook. Preheat the skillet before you are done slicing the vegetables. Prepare the dressing while the vegetables are cooking. Slice the avocado right before serving to prevent discoloration.

senate bean soup bowl (page 140)

eight | soup bowls

Cooking up a pot of soup can be as simple as simmering a few vegetables in a prepared vegetable broth. For the purpose of a complete meal, however, bowl soups require heartiness and bulk, which you'll find in all my soups. These bowls are nutritious and satisfying. Even during the summer, a substantial soup should be one that feels like a complete meal. My Chicken-Free Noodle Soup can be ready in under thirty minutes, but it tastes like it's been cooking all day. It's full of beans, noodles, vegetables, and loads of flavor. That is the pattern throughout the chapter: great soups and layers of flavor, but you spend just minutes in the kitchen. Try the Pasta e Fagioli, an Italian classic, or the Vietnamese Pho, a traditional noodle soup flavored with anise and basil. Mmm! So good and satisfying!

tortilla soup bowl

SERVES 4 | GF, SF

This version of tortilla soup is slightly spicy, very filling, and customizable, depending on the toppings you choose. Most often, the tortillas are added to the bottom of the bowl with soup ladled over them, but if you are more into crispy chips, wait to add the tortilla chips as a garnish.

SAUCE

1/4 cup raw cashew pieces

1/4 cup water

2 tablespoons coarsely chopped cilantro

2 teaspoons fresh lime juice

Sea salt and black pepper, to taste

BEANS

6 cups vegetable broth

5 sprigs cilantro

1 sprig fresh oregano

2 cups cooked black beans

2 cups cooked pinto beans

1 cup corn kernels

1 teaspoon sea salt

VEGETABLES

2 medium Roma tomatoes, coarsely chopped

1 medium onion, coarsely chopped

4 garlic cloves, coarsely chopped

2 teaspoons Chipotle Purée (page 14)

2 cups tortilla chips

1 ripe Hass avocado, pitted and peeled, coarsely chopped (optional)

1 jalapeño, seeded and minced (optional)

2 tablespoons minced cilantro (optional)

SUBSTITUTION: Omit the sauce ingredients and directions and instead serve the soup with shredded vegan cheese.

SAUCE: Combine the cashews with enough water to cover in a small saucepan. Cover, bring to boil, then reduce the heat to medium and simmer for 5 minutes. Set aside for 5 minutes, drain and rinse. Transfer to a small blender. Add the 1/4 cup water, cilantro, lime, salt and black pepper. Blend until smooth as possible and set aside.

BEANS: Combine the broth, cilantro, oregano, beans, corn, and salt in a large pot over high heat. Cover and bring to boil, reduce to simmer over medium heat and cook until needed.

VEGETABLES: Combine the tomato, onion, garlic, and chipotle in a food processor. Pulse until finely minced. Transfer to a large skillet and cook over medium-high heat, stirring frequently, until the vegetables are dry, about 10 minutes. Add the vegetables to the broth. Cook the soup for another 5 minutes to meld flavors. Taste and adjust seasoning with salt and black pepper.

Serve the soup in bowls garnished with sauce, tortilla chips, avocado, jalapeño, and cilantro, if using.

 QUICK TIPS: Begin heating the broth while you assemble the broth ingredients. Chop the vegetables into large pieces because the food processor will be doing most of the work. Finish making the sauce while the vegetables are cooking.

green and white chili bowl

SERVES 4 TO 6 | GF, SF

Red chili is all the rage, but its seldom-made cousin—green and white chili—is just as flavorful, perhaps more so. This chili is full of hominy (dried and treated maize), fresh green chiles, and two kinds of white beans. If you cannot find hominy, use thawed corn kernels instead.

BEANS

- 4 cups vegetable broth
- 1 teaspoon dried oregano
- 1/2 teaspoon sea salt
- 4 cups cooked cannellini beans
- 2 (15-ounce) cans white hominy, rinsed and drained
- 2 cups cooked chickpeas

VEGETABLES

- 4 Anaheim peppers, coarsely chopped
- 1 jalapeño, coarsely chopped
- 1 medium onion, coarsely chopped
- 6 garlic cloves, crushed
- 1 tablespoon grapeseed oil
- 2 teaspoons ground cumin
- 8 ounces fresh spinach, tough stems removed, coarsely chopped
- Sea salt and black pepper, to taste
- 2 tablespoons fresh lime juice
- 1/4 cup coarsely chopped cilantro
- 1 ripe Hass avocado, pitted, peeled, and coarsely chopped (optional)

SUBSTITUTION: Substitute 4 cups corn kernels for the hominy. Substitute pinto beans for the chickpeas. Substitute 3 green bell peppers for the Anaheim peppers.

BEANS: Combine the broth, oregano, salt, cannellini, hominy, and chickpeas in a large pot. Cover and bring to a boil over high heat, reduce to simmer and cook until needed.

VEGETABLES: Add the peppers, onion, and garlic to a food processor. Pulse until minced. Heat the oil in a large pot over high heat. Add the minced vegetables and cumin and cook until the mixture is dry, about 8 minutes, stirring often.

Add the broth and beans to the sautéed vegetables and simmer until the flavors combine, about 5 minutes. Add the spinach and cook until tender. Taste and adjust seasoning with salt and black pepper. Stir in the lime juice and cilantro. Serve with the avocado, if using.

QUICK TIPS: Chop the peppers and onion into large pieces, since the food processor will be doing most of the work.

gumbo bowl with okra and kidney beans

SERVES 4 | SF

Gumbo's distinct flavor comes from the roux, a sauce mixture of fat and flour that is cooked first in the bottom of the pot. The darker the roux, the more flavor it has. However, the long cooking time required reduces the thickening ability of the roux. For that reason, gumbo is thickened with either okra or filé powder (ground sassafras leaves). The challenge is to make a roux worthy of a gumbo, but accomplish it much faster.

RICE

- 2 1/4 cups water
- 1 1/2 cups long-grain white rice
- 1/2 teaspoon sea salt

ROUX

- 3 tablespoons grapeseed oil
- 6 tablespoons whole-wheat pastry flour or all-purpose flour
- 4 cups vegetable broth

SOUP

- 1 teaspoon grapeseed oil
- 2 bay leaves
- 1 teaspoon fresh or dried thyme
- 1 teaspoon dry mustard
- 1/4 teaspoon red pepper flakes
- 1/4 teaspoon ground allspice
- 1 (10-ounce) bag frozen sliced okra, not thawed
- 1 medium onion, finely chopped
- 1 celery rib, finely chopped
- 1 green bell pepper, finely chopped
- 4 garlic cloves, minced
- 1 teaspoon dulse flakes
- 1 teaspoon sea salt
- 1/2 teaspoon black pepper
- 4 cups cooked kidney beans
- 2 scallions, finely chopped

SUBSTITUTION: Substitute 30-Minute Brown Rice (page 16) for the white rice if you have a few additional minutes.

RICE: Combine the water, rice and salt in a medium saucepan. Cover and bring to boil over medium-high heat. Reduce to simmer over low heat and cook for 15 minutes. Remove from the heat and set aside, still covered, for 10 minutes to steam. Fluff before serving.

ROUX: Heat the oil in a medium saucepan over medium heat. Stir in the flour and cook, stirring frequently with a wooden spoon, until the roux is dark chocolate brown, 10 to 15 minutes. If the roux starts smoking, remove the pan from the heat, stir well and return to the heat. Add the broth 1 cup at a time, whisking after the addition of each cup. Bring to a boil and reduce to a simmer. Simmer, covered, until needed.

SOUP: Heat the oil in a large pot over medium-high heat. Add the bay leaves, thyme, mustard, red pepper flakes, allspice, and frozen okra. Stir well and cook for 3 to 5 minutes. Add the onion, celery, bell pepper, garlic, dulse, salt, and pepper to the pot. Cook, stirring, until the vegetables soften, about 8 minutes. Add the roux-broth mixture. Add the beans and cook until the flavors are combined and the soup thickens, 5 to 10 minutes. Taste and adjust seasoning with salt and pepper.

Serve the gumbo in bowls, add rice to the gumbo, and sprinkle with scallions.

QUICK TIPS: No need to thaw the okra before cooking. While the okra is cooking, chop the vegetables near the stove. Add the vegetables to the pot as soon as they are chopped; no need to wait to add everything at once. Chop the scallions while the soup thickens.

pho bowl with seitan

SERVES 4 | GFO, SFO

The backbone of this soup is the broth. Pho is a traditional and popular Vietnamese soup that is eaten at any time, morning, noon, or night. It is important that this flavorful soup be served piping hot.

BASE

- 8 cups water
- 1 teaspoon grapeseed oil
- 1/2 cup dried shiitake mushrooms
- 1 medium kohlrabi or 8 ounces broccoli stems, unpeeled, cut into 1-inch cubes
- 4 medium carrots, cut into 1/2-inch slices
- 2 cups red radishes (about 15), cut in half
- 4 garlic cloves
- 2 medium onions, unpeeled, cut into quarters
- 1 (4-inch) piece ginger, unpeeled, cut into 1/4-inch thick slices on the bias

SPICES

- 1 tablespoon whole peppercorns
- 1 tablespoon coriander seeds
- 1 teaspoon fennel seeds
- 2 black cardamom pods
- 1 stick cinnamon
- 8 whole cloves
- 5 star anise

SOUP

- 1 pound Slow-Simmered Seitan (page 11), or store-bought seitan cut into 1/2-inch thick slices
- 1 teaspoon grapeseed oil
- 2 teaspoons reduced-sodium tamari
- 1 1/2 teaspoons natural sugar
- 2 teaspoons sea salt
- 1 medium carrot, cut into julienne slices
- 8 ounces bok choy, coarsely chopped
- 4 ounces thick brown rice noodles or rice sticks
- 1/2 cup Thai basil, Genoese basil or cilantro
- 2 scallions, minced
- Hoisin and sriracha for serving

BASE: Heat the water in a large pot over high heat. Add the oil, mushrooms, kohlrabi, carrots, radishes, and garlic. Cover, bring to boil and reduce to simmer over medium heat until needed, about 20 minutes. Heat a grill pan or cast iron skillet over medium-high heat. Add the onion and ginger slices. Grill until charred, about 4 minutes per side. Transfer the grilled vegetables to the simmering broth.

SPICES: Preheat a small skillet over medium heat. Add the peppercorns, coriander, fennel, cardamom, cinnamon, clove, and star anise. Toast the spices until fragrant and golden, about 3 minutes, stirring frequently. Transfer the spices to the simmering broth.

SOUP: Toss the seitan with the oil. Grill or sauté the seitan until grill marks appear, about 1 minute per side. Set aside.

After about 20 minutes of simmering, strain the broth into a large bowl using a fine-mesh strainer. Discard the strained spices and vegetables and transfer the broth back to the pot. Season the soup with the tamari, sugar and salt. Taste and adjust seasoning. Add the carrot and bok choy. Simmer over medium heat until the vegetables are tender and the soup is piping hot, about 2 minutes.

Prepare the noodles by cooking in a medium saucepan of boiling water until tender, about 3 minutes, stirring constantly to wash away any starch. Drain well. Serve the soup in warmed bowls with the noodles and seitan. Garnish with herbs and scallions. Serve with hoisin and sriracha.

 QUICK TIPS: Heat the large pot with the water, then preheat the skillet and grill pan. Measure the ingredients into the skillet to toast.

GLUTEN-FREE OPTION: Replace the seitan with baked tofu.

SOY-FREE OPTION: Substitute coconut aminos with a few pinches of sea salt for the tamari.

everyday dal with potato cakes

SERVES 4 | GFO, SF

A dal is an Indian soup or stew made of split lentils. The dal is flavored with some spices as it cooks, but the real flavor comes at the end with the addition of tempered spices and herbs. There are several Indian dishes that serve potato cakes with a dal poured over them, but I recommend dipping the cakes into the dal to keep them crisp throughout the meal.

DAL

- 4 cups water
- 1 1/2 cups red lentils (masoor dal), picked over and rinsed
- 1/2 medium ripe tomato, coarsely chopped
- 1/4 teaspoon ground turmeric

POTATO CAKES

- 1 pound Yukon Gold or other waxy potatoes (about 4 medium), peeled and cut into 1-inch chunks
- 1 1/2 teaspoons sea salt
- 2 teaspoons grapeseed oil, plus more as needed
- 1 medium carrot, grated
- 1/2 medium onion, finely chopped
- 4 garlic cloves, minced
- 1/4 cup whole-wheat pastry flour or all-purpose flour
- Sea salt and black pepper, to taste

SPICES

- 1 tablespoon grapeseed oil
- 1 tablespoon cumin seeds
- 1 tablespoon mustard seeds, preferably black mustard seeds
- 1 teaspoon red pepper flakes
- 5 curry leaves (optional)
- 1/2 teaspoon asafoetida (optional)
- 4 garlic cloves, minced
- 1/2 medium ripe tomato, finely chopped
- 6 cups fresh baby spinach
- Sea salt and black pepper, to taste

GLUTEN-FREE OPTION: Substitute 2 tablespoons arrowroot starch or organic cornstarch for the flour.

DAL: Combine the water, dal, tomato, and turmeric in a medium saucepan. Cover, bring to boil and reduce to simmer over medium heat. Partially cover and cook until tender, about 20 minutes. Using a whisk, whip the dal until smooth.

POTATO CAKES: Combine the potato, salt, and enough water to cover in a medium saucepan. Bring to boil over high heat, reduce to medium, and cook until knife-tender; do not overcook. Drain and transfer to a bowl. Mash the potato. Set aside.

Heat 2 teaspoons oil in a large skillet over medium heat. Stir in the carrot and onion. Cover and cook until softened, about 5 minutes. Stir in the garlic and cook until fragrant, about 1 minute. Add the carrot mixture to the mashed potatoes. Add the flour and season with salt and pepper and mix well. Heat about 1 tablespoon oil in a large skillet over medium heat. Divide the mashed potato mixture into 1/4 cup portions and form each portion into a patty about 1-inch thick. Cook the patties until golden brown, about 4 minutes per side.

SPICES: Heat the oil in a small or medium skillet over medium heat. Add the cumin, mustard, red pepper flakes, curry leaves and asafoetida, if using. Cook, stirring, until the mustard seeds begin to pop. Add the garlic and cook until fragrant, 30 seconds. Add the tomato and cook until it starts breaking down, about 2 minutes. Add the tomato mixture to the whipped dal. Add the spinach to the dal and simmer until the spinach is tender, about 2 minutes. Taste and adjust seasoning with salt and pepper. Serve the dal in bowls with the potato cakes.

 QUICK TIPS: Heat the water while you rinse and pick over the dal. Chop the whole tomato; you will need it all. Heat the water for the potatoes before peeling the potatoes. Preheat the skillet when you are almost done grating the carrot and onion. Toast the spices while the potatoes sauté.

hearty sambar bowl

SERVES 4 | GF, SF

Sambar is an Indian soup of lentils and vegetables that is flavored with tamarind, a tart-sour fruit commonly used in African and Asian cuisine. This soup is traditionally eaten with Chapatis (page 12), idli, or rice. It is somewhat spicy and somewhat tart, which is balanced by the neutral flatbread or rice.

RICE

- 1 1/2 cups water
- 1/2 teaspoon sea salt
- 1 cup long-grain white rice

SOUP

- 3 cups water
- 1 cup red dal (masoor dal), picked over and rinsed
- 1 small onion, coarsely chopped

VEGETABLES

- 3 cups water
- 1 medium bell pepper, coarsely chopped
- 1 medium tomato, coarsely chopped
- 2 cups coarsely chopped vegetable, such as cauliflower, zucchini, green beans
- 1 tablespoon tamarind concentrate
- Sea salt and black pepper

SAMBAR MASALA POWDER

- 1 tablespoon coriander seeds
- 1 teaspoon cumin seeds
- 1 teaspoon fenugreek seeds
- 1 teaspoon sea salt
- 1 teaspoon red pepper flakes
- 1/4 teaspoon ground turmeric

TEMPERING

- 1 tablespoon grapeseed oil
- 1 teaspoon mustard seeds
- 8 to 10 curry leaves
- 1/2 teaspoon asafoetida

SUBSTITUTIONS: Substitute 30-Minute Brown Rice (page 16) for the white rice. Use about 2 tablespoons commercial sambar masala instead of homemade.

RICE: Heat the water and salt in a small saucepan over high heat. Rinse the rice in two changes of fresh water and add to the pan. When the water is bubbling on the sides of the pot cover the pot, reduce the heat to low and cook for 15 minutes. Remove from the heat and set aside for 10 minutes to steam. Fluff with a fork before serving.

SOUP: Combine the water, dal, and onion in a medium saucepan and bring to boil. Reduce to a simmer and cook until the dal is falling apart, about 20 minutes. When the dal is cooked, use a whisk to blend completely and add it to the vegetables.

VEGETABLES: Combine the water, bell pepper, tomato, and chopped vegetables in a large pot over high heat. Bring to boil and reduce to simmer over medium heat. Cook, covered, until the vegetables are tender, about 10 minutes. Add the sambar powder and stir. Add the tamarind and season the soup with salt and black pepper. Cook the soup for a few more minutes to meld the flavors.

SAMBAR MASALA POWDER: Preheat a small skillet over medium heat. Add the coriander, cumin, and fenugreek seeds. Stir and cook until the seeds are golden, about 3 minutes. Transfer to a small blender or spice grinder along with the salt, red pepper flakes and turmeric. Grind to a very fine powder.

TEMPERING: Heat the oil in a small skillet over medium heat. Add the mustard seeds and cook until they begin to pop. Add the curry leaves and asafoetida. Stir and cook until fragrant, 30 seconds, then stir into the sambar. To serve, spoon the rice into bowls and top with the sambar.

QUICK TIPS: Begin by heating the water for the rice and the soup. Rinse the rice and the lentils using the strainer. Begin cooking the lentils and then chop the vegetables beginning with the onion. Chop the rest of the vegetables while the lentils cook. Prepare the sambar powder. Lastly, prepare the tempering.

hungarian cauliflower soup bowl

SERVES 4 | SF

My mom used to make this soup almost monthly. She would use cauliflower or kohlrabi, a vegetable cross between a turnip and a cabbage. Kohlrabi takes a bit longer to cook than cauliflower, but the unique flavor is well worth the extra few minutes. Freekeh is not a traditional addition, but it brings wholesomeness and protein to the soup.

BROTH

- 5 cups vegetable broth
- 2/3 cup cracked freekeh
- 2 teaspoons sea salt
- 1 bay leaf

ROUX

- 2 tablespoons grapeseed oil
- 1 small onion, finely chopped
- 6 tablespoons whole-wheat pastry flour or all-purpose flour
- 2 cups unsweetened plain almond, soy, or rice milk
- 1 teaspoon Hungarian paprika

VEGETABLES

- 1 small head cauliflower, cut into small florets
- 1 cup frozen green peas, rinsed to thaw
- 2 teaspoons white wine vinegar
- 3/4 cup minced parsley
- Sea salt and black pepper, to taste

SUBSTITUTIONS: Substitute 1 1/2 pounds kohlrabi for the cauliflower. Peel the kohlrabi and chop into 1/2-inch dice. Substitute cracked bulgur for the freekeh.

BROTH: Combine the broth, freekeh, salt, and bay leaf in a large pot over high heat. Cover, bring to boil and reduce to simmer over medium heat. Cook until the freekeh is partially cooked, 10 minutes, or until needed.

ROUX: Heat the oil in a medium saucepan over medium heat. Add the onion, cover, and cook until tender, 5 minutes, stirring occasionally. Add the flour and cook until golden, continuously stirring, for 2 minutes. Add 1/2 cup of the milk and stir using a whisk until the roux is smooth. Add another 1/2 cup of the milk and stir until smooth. Add the rest of the milk and paprika. Bring to a simmer and transfer to the soup broth.

VEGETABLES: Add the cauliflower to the soup and cook until the freekeh and cauliflower are tender, about 8 minutes. Remove and discard the bay leaf. Add the peas, vinegar and parsley, stir and adjust seasoning with salt and black pepper. Serve in bowls.

QUICK TIPS: Prepare the cauliflower while the onions cook. Prepare the parsley while the cauliflower cooks. Thaw the peas quickly in a fine-mesh strainer in a bowl of water.

PREPARING KOHLRABI: Using a sharp knife, trim off the top and bottom of the kohlrabi and then peel off the tough skin.

pepper pot soup bowl
with spinner dumplings

SERVES 4 | GFO, SF

Pepper Pot Soup hails from the Caribbean. According to legend, it was brought to Philadelphia during the American Revolutionary War. Philadelphia still serves a version of Pepper Pot Soup, omitting the coconut milk. Since I am fond of original recipes, my version of this Jamaican soup is complete with coconut milk and Scotch Bonnet chiles. For those less inclined to spice, the soup is just as fantastic with no heat at all. Spinner dumplings are made by rolling, or spinning, dough between the flat palms of the hands.

BROTH

- 4 cups vegetable broth
- 2 cups cooked kidney beans
- 8 ounces collard greens, tough stems removed, coarsely chopped
- 1 (1-inch) piece ginger, finely grated
- 1/2 scotch bonnet or habanero chile
- 2 bay leaves
- 1 teaspoon ground allspice
- 1 teaspoon fresh or dried thyme
- 1 teaspoon sea salt
- Black pepper, to taste

SAUTÉ

- 1 tablespoon olive oil
- 1 medium onion, finely chopped
- 2 garlic cloves, minced
- 1 medium sweet potato, peeled and cut into 1-inch dice
- 5 scallions, minced
- 1 (14-ounce) can coconut milk

DUMPLINGS

- 1/2 cup whole-wheat pastry flour or all-purpose flour
- 1/2 teaspoon sea salt
- 2 1/2 tablespoons cold water

GLUTEN-FREE OPTION: Add 1 cup cooked gluten-free pasta to the finished soup instead of making the dumplings.

BROTH: Combine the broth, beans, collards, ginger, scotch bonnet, bay leaves, allspice, thyme, salt, and black pepper in a medium saucepan. Cover and bring to boil, then reduce the heat to a simmer and cook until needed, about 10 minutes.

SAUTÉ: Heat the oil in a large pot over medium-high heat. Add the onion, cover and cook, stirring occasionally, until lightly golden, about 5 minutes. Stir in the garlic and cook for 30 seconds. Add the potato, scallions and the broth with the beans. Bring to a boil and reduce to simmer over medium heat. Cook, covered, until the potatoes and collards are tender, about 5 minutes. Stir in the coconut milk and bring back to a simmer.

DUMPLINGS: Combine the flour and salt in a small bowl. Stir in the water and knead the dough for a few minutes. Form the dough into a log about 1-inch wide. Cut the log into 1/8-inch slices. Holding a slice of dough between the flat palms of your hands, roll it into a thin log. Drop the dough into the simmering broth. Repeat until all the pieces are rolled. Stir well and cook until the dumplings are tender, 2 to 3 minutes.

Taste and adjust seasoning. Remove and discard the bay leaves and habanero and serve in bowls.

QUICK TIPS: Bring the broth to a boil as you add the broth ingredients. Prepare the sweet potato while the onion cooks. Prepare the dough for the dumplings while the soup returns to a simmer after you add the coconut milk.

pasta e fagioli bowl

SERVES 4 | GFO, SFO

Pasta e fagioli shows up in many cookbooks, but this one is not your run-of-the-mill pasta and beans soup. This soup has a wonderful kick because of the addition of watercress, a peppery-tasting green. If you can't find watercress, arugula is an adequate stand-in. Only add the pasta to the soup if you are serving it right away, otherwise the pasta will soak up all the soup as it sits. (See photo on page vi.)

SOUP

- 6 cups vegetable broth
- 2 cups cooked kidney beans
- 2 cups cooked cannellini beans, mashed
- 1 teaspoon fresh or 1/2 teaspoon dried thyme
- 1 teaspoon dried oregano
- 1/2 teaspoon sea salt
- 1/4 teaspoon red pepper flakes
- 1 bay leaf

VEGETABLES

- 1 tablespoon toasted sesame oil
- 1 teaspoon olive oil
- 1 medium onion, finely chopped
- 2 celery ribs, finely chopped
- 4 garlic cloves, minced
- 2 tablespoons tomato paste

PASTA

- 3/4 cup small pasta, such as shells
- 4 cups watercress or baby arugula
- 1/4 cup finely chopped parsley
- 1 tablespoon white miso
- Black pepper

GLUTEN-FREE OPTION: Instead of using the dried wheat pasta, add 1 1/2 cups cooked gluten-free pasta just before serving.

SOY-FREE OPTION: Replace the white miso with chickpea miso.

SOUP: Combine the broth, beans, thyme, oregano, salt, red pepper flakes, and bay leaf in a large pot over high heat. Bring to boil, reduce to simmer over medium heat and cook until needed.

VEGETABLES: Heat the oils in a large skillet over medium heat. Add the onion, cover the skillet and cook until the onion is soft, about 3 minutes. Add the celery and garlic and continue to cook, uncovered, until the celery is tender, about 4 more minutes. Stir in the tomato paste and cook until the paste turns darker, about 30 seconds. Transfer the mixture to the soup and simmer for 5 minutes.

PASTA: Stir in the pasta and cook until tender, 8 to 10 minutes. Add the watercress and parsley and remove the soup from the heat. Transfer 1/2 cup of the soup broth into a small bowl and add the miso, stirring until dissolved. Stir the miso mixture into the soup. Remove and discard the bay leaf. Taste and adjust seasoning with salt and black pepper. Serve.

QUICK TIPS: Begin by heating the broth for the soup and add the soup ingredients as they become ready. Chop the celery and garlic while the onion cooks. Clean and chop the watercress and parsley while the pasta cooks.

figgy porridge bowl (page 158)

nine | breakfast bowls

Many breakfast foods are served in a bowl, ranging from cold cereals to oatmeal, but these recipes will have you craving breakfast bowls at any time of day. In this chapter, you'll find twists on old classics as well as creative new bowls. Although these recipes are not veggie heavy—some having no vegetables at all, such as the Cinnamon Toast Oatmeal—rest assured that these bowls will start your day on the right track. These globally friendly bowls will take you to Asia and Europe and back to North America, where you can break your fast with a quick Breakfast Quinoa (picture a sweet variation of the beloved South American staple). No cutting corners with these bowl dishes! Variety is the spice of life, and you will find plenty of that in this chapter.

sin huevos rancheros bowl

SERVES 4 | SFO, GF

This is a popular Mexican breakfast dish of corn tortillas, poached eggs, and ranchero sauce. In this version, tofu is simmered in the spicy ranchero sauce before being added to the lightly fried tortillas. The avocado provides the creamy texture and ties together the Latin American flavors.

BEANS

- 2 cups cooked black beans
- 1 garlic clove, crushed
- 1/2 cup water
- 1 teaspoon ground cumin
- 1/2 teaspoon dried oregano
- 1/4 teaspoon sea salt

TOFU

- 1 tablespoon olive oil
- 8 (3-inch) corn tortillas or 4 (5-inch) corn tortillas, cut in half
- 1 (10 ounce) package super-firm tofu, patted dry and cut into 1/4-inch slices
- Sea salt and black pepper

RANCHERO SAUCE

- 1 tablespoon olive oil
- 1 medium onion, finely chopped
- 4 garlic cloves, finely minced
- 1 teaspoon ground cumin
- 1/2 teaspoon dried oregano
- 1 (28-ounce) can whole tomatoes, drained (10 peeled Roma tomatoes)
- 1 to 2 serrano chiles, coarsely chopped
- 3/4 cup lightly-packed cilantro
- Sea salt and black pepper

GARNISH

- 1 ripe Hass avocado, pitted, peeled, and cut into 1/2- inch slices
- Cilantro leaves
- Lime slices
- Serrano chile slices (optional)
- 2 tablespoons crumbled vegan nut cheese (optional)

BEANS: Combine the beans, garlic, water, cumin, oregano, and salt in a medium saucepan over medium heat. Bring to boil, reduce to medium-low and simmer until needed. Mash the beans, if desired, before serving.

TOFU: Heat the oil in a large skillet over medium heat until it shimmers. Add the tortillas and cook until soft and pliable, about 30 seconds per side. Transfer the tortillas to a folded kitchen towel or tortilla warmer lined with a paper towel, cover and keep warm. Add 1 teaspoon oil to the skillet, if needed. Add the tofu and cook until golden, about 4 minutes per side. Season with salt and pepper. Remove and set aside.

SAUCE: Heat the oil in the large skillet over medium heat. Add the onion and garlic, cover and cook until caramelized, 8 to 10 minutes, stirring occasionally. Season with cumin, oregano, and salt. Add the tomatoes and serrano to a food processor and process. Add the cilantro and pulse to mince. Transfer the tomato mixture to the skillet. Add the tofu slices and cook, uncovered, until the sauce thickens, 6 to 8 minutes, stirring occasionally. Adjust seasoning with salt and pepper.

ASSEMBLY: Place a tortilla on the bottom of a shallow bowl, top with beans and ranchero sauce and another tortilla. Add 2 to 3 slices of tofu and more ranchero sauce. Garnish with slices of avocado, cilantro, lime, serrano, and cheese, if using.

QUICK TIPS: Mince the onion and garlic in the food processor before processing the tomatoes. Since the food processor will be doing most of the work, you can chop the onion and serrano into large pieces.

SOY-FREE OPTION: Omit the tofu and increase the beans to 3 cups and the water to 3/4 cup; leave some beans whole to add texture to the final dish.

cinnamon toast oatmeal bowl

SERVES 4 | GF, SF

A taste of this oatmeal will transport you back to childhood when you buttered a piece of toast and liberally added sugar and cinnamon. The oatmeal is dotted with quinoa and has just enough cinnamon. The streusel topping adds texture to the bowl, and the final drizzle of maple syrup lets you control the sweetness. If you are sensitive to gluten, make sure you use gluten-free oats.

STREUSEL

- 2 tablespoons natural sugar
- 1 tablespoon grapeseed oil
- 1 tablespoon pure maple syrup
- 1 teaspoon ground cinnamon
- 1/4 teaspoon fresh ground nutmeg
- Pinch salt
- 1/2 cup sliced raw almonds
- 1/4 cup rolled oats

OATMEAL

- 3 cups nondairy milk
- 1/4 cup quinoa, well rinsed
- 1 teaspoon ground cinnamon
- Pinch sea salt
- 1 1/4 cups rolled oats
- 1/4 cup minced dried apricots
- 1 teaspoon pure vanilla extract
- 2 tablespoons maple syrup, plus more for garnish

STREUSEL: Preheat the oven to 350°F. Combine the sugar, oil, syrup, cinnamon, nutmeg, and salt in a medium bowl. Add the almonds and oats. Mix well and transfer to a baking sheet. Bake until crisp, stirring halfway through, about 15 minutes. Set aside to cool.

OATMEAL: Heat the milk, quinoa, cinnamon, and salt in a medium saucepan over high heat. Bring to boil, reduce to simmer over medium-low heat and add the oats and apricots. Cook for 10 minutes, stirring occasionally. Cover and simmer over low heat until the quinoa is tender, about 5 more minutes. Remove from the heat and set aside for 5 minutes. Stir in the vanilla and maple syrup. Stir in 1/2 cup of the streusel.

ASSEMBLY: Serve the oatmeal garnished with the streusel and maple syrup.

QUICK TIPS: Begin heating the milk and quinoa before preparing the topping.

chocolate-cherry granola bowl
with almonds

MAKE 4 CUPS | GF, SF

Cherry loves chocolate, and this quick and low-fat granola is definitely a winning breakfast. Serve over yogurt or with non-dairy milk, or do what my kids do and eat it straight out of the jar. This recipe successfully doubles, but it will need an extra 5 to 10 minutes baking time. If you are sensitive to gluten, make sure you use gluten-free oats.

BASE

1 cup rolled oats

1/2 cup slivered raw almonds

MIX-INS

6 tablespoons cherry fruit spread

2 tablespoons pure maple syrup

1 teaspoon pure vanilla extract

2 tablespoons unsweetened cocoa powder

1/2 cup dried tart cherries

1/2 cup brown rice cereal

Vegan yogurt

Nondairy milk

BASE: Preheat the oven to 325°F. Combine the oats and almonds on a large baking sheet and bake until toasted, about 10 minutes, stirring after 5 minutes.

MIX-INS: Combine the fruit spread, syrup, vanilla, and cocoa powder in a medium bowl. Add the toasted oats and nuts, cherries, and cereal and mix well. Transfer back to the baking sheet and bake for 15 minutes, stirring every 5 minutes. Cool completely before storing in an airtight container, where it will keep for up to a month.

Serve the granola in bowls on top of vegan yogurt, or serve topped with nondairy milk.

creamed chipped hash bowl

My husband grew up loving the breakfast dish affectionately termed SOS, and asked me to throw my spin on the classic cream chipped beef recipe. Here is my version, which uses tempeh in the gravy and adds a quick potato hash.

GRAVY

- 1 tablespoon toasted sesame oil
- 1 medium onion, finely chopped
- 1/4 teaspoon red pepper flakes
- 1 tablespoon grapeseed oil
- 8 ounce tempeh, finely chopped
- 1/4 cup whole-wheat pastry or all-purpose flour
- 1 cup vegetable broth
- 2 cups unsweetened plain nondairy milk
- 1 teaspoon Dijon mustard
- 1/2 teaspoon smoked paprika
- Sea salt and black pepper
- 8 ounces chard, tough stems removed, coarsely chopped

HASH

- 2 tablespoons grapeseed oil
- 1 pound Yukon Gold or other waxy potatoes, peeled and cut into 1/4-inch dice
- Sea salt and black pepper
- 4 slices thick bread, toasted and cut into large chunks

SOY-FREE OPTION: Replace the tempeh with 8 ounces of very thinly sliced seitan. Add enough grapeseed oil to the skillet to prevent the seitan from sticking and cook until crispy, about 10 minutes.

SUBSTITUTION: If needed, substitute spinach for the chard. Collards or kale will overwhelm the flavors.

GRAVY: Heat the sesame oil in a large skillet over medium heat. Add the onion and red pepper flakes. Cover and cook until softened, about 5 minutes, stirring occasionally. Add the grapeseed oil and tempeh and cook until golden brown, about 10 minutes, stirring occasionally.

Add the flour, stir and cook until it smells nutty, about 2 minutes. Stir in the broth and simmer until thickened. Add the milk, mustard, paprika, salt and black pepper. Bring to simmer, add the chard and cook until the chard is tender and the gravy has thickened, about 5 minutes.

HASH: Heat the oil in a separate large skillet over medium heat. Add the potatoes and cook until golden and tender, about 20 minutes, stirring as needed. If the potatoes are sticking too much, they are not ready to be turned; cook a bit longer before trying to turn. Season with salt and black pepper.

ASSEMBLY: Layer the toast in the bottom of bowls, add the hash, and smother with the gravy.

QUICK TIPS: Chop the tempeh while the onion cooks. Chop the chard and begin preparing the potatoes while the tempeh cooks. If the gravy is ready before the potatoes, cover it to keep it warm over low heat.

quinoa breakfast bowl

SERVES 4 | GF, SF

Quinoa should be included in your breakfast rotation. It is hearty, nutritious and easy to make. It also happens to be wonderful in sweet applications. Here it is paired with pears, oranges and green cardamom, another delicious flavor affinity.

QUINOA

- 1 1/2 cups nondairy milk
- 1 tablespoon pure maple syrup
- 1 cup quinoa, well rinsed
- 4 green cardamom pods
- 1 (2-inch) piece orange zest, no white pith

FRUIT AND NUTS

- 1 teaspoon grapeseed oil
- 1/2 cup chopped nuts, such as hazelnut, pistachio, or almond
- 2 ripe pears, cut into 1/2-inch dice
- 1 tablespoon maple syrup
- Pinch salt
- 1 large orange, segmented and chopped or 2 tangerines, segmented

QUINOA: Combine the milk, syrup, quinoa, cardamom, and zest in a medium saucepan over high heat. Bring to boil and reduce to simmer, taking care not to let it boil over. Simmer, partly covered, for 10 minutes. Cover tightly and continue to cook for 10 more minutes. Remove from heat and set aside for 5 minutes to steam.

FRUIT AND NUTS: Heat the oil in a small saucepan over medium heat. Add the nuts and cook, stirring often, until they are toasted, about 3 minutes. Remove the nuts from the heat and set aside. Add the pears, syrup, and salt to the pan and cook, stirring, until the pear is glazed, about 3 minutes. Set aside.

ASSEMBLY: Fluff the quinoa, remove the zest and cardamom and discard. Stir in the pears, nuts, and oranges. Serve in bowls.

QUICK TIPS: Begin preparing the topping when the quinoa is midway through cooking.

figgy porridge bowl

SERVES 4 | GF, SF

Candied figs, dried fruit, nuts, and coconut top this semi-sweet corn porridge. The candied topping can be prepared ahead of time and stored for up to a month in an airtight container. It takes mere moments to assemble this dish, even if the topping is not prepared in advance. (See photo on page 148.)

TOPPING

- 1 cup coarsely chopped raw pecans, cashews or walnuts
- 1 cup coarsely chopped dried figs, stems removed
- 1/2 cup coarsely chopped dried apples, dried apricots or dried cherries
- 3 tablespoons pure maple syrup
- 1/4 teaspoon ground cinnamon
- Pinch salt
- 1/2 cup dried shredded coconut (optional)

PORRIDGE

- 1 cup water
- 1/2 cup coarsely chopped dried figs, stems removed
- 1 tablespoon pure maple syrup, plus more for garnish
- 1/4 teaspoon ground cinnamon
- 3/4 cup polenta or medium-ground cornmeal
- 2 cups nondairy milk, divided
- 1 teaspoon pure vanilla extract

SUBSTITUTION: Substitute apricots or prunes for the figs in both the topping and porridge.

TOPPING: Preheat the oven to 375°F. Combine the nuts, figs, apples, syrup, cinnamon and salt on a metal baking sheet lined with parchment paper or a silicone baking mat. Bake the topping until most of the syrup is absorbed, about 15 minutes, stirring midway through baking. If using coconut flakes, stir them in during the last 2 minutes of baking. Remove from the oven and set aside to cool and harden. When completely cool, store in an airtight container for up to 1 month.

PORRIDGE: Combine the water, figs, syrup and cinnamon in a medium saucepan over high heat. Bring to boil and whisk in the polenta. Add 1 1/2 cups of milk and reduce the heat to medium-low. Cook, stirring occasionally, until the polenta is tender, 10 to 15 minutes. Stir in the remaining 1/2 cup of milk if the polenta is too thick. Stir in the vanilla and serve the porridge in bowls with the candied topping and garnished with maple syrup, if desired.

seitan-bacon hash bowl
with brussels sprouts

SERVES 2 TO 3 | GFO, SFO

Give me potatoes, seitan, and Brussels sprouts for breakfast, and I'm a happy woman. In this recipe, the seitan is cooked until crisp and added to the hash. Quick and easy, breakfast in a flash. If your seitan is particularly moist, give it a gentle squeeze to remove excess liquid.

HASH

- 1 tablespoon grapeseed oil
- 1 medium onion, finely chopped
- 1 medium carrot, cut into 1/2-inch dice
- 1 pound (2 medium) russet potatoes, peeled and cut into 1/2-inch dice
- 8 ounces Brussels sprouts, trimmed and halved, quartered if sprouts are large
- 1 teaspoon fresh or dried thyme
- 1 teaspoon sea salt
- 3/4 cup vegetable broth, divided
- Red pepper flakes and black pepper

SEITAN

- 1 tablespoon grapeseed oil, plus more as needed
- 8 ounces Slow-Simmered Seitan (page 11) or store-bought seitan, cut into 1/4-inch thick strips
- 1 tablespoon reduced-sodium tamari
- 1 teaspoon smoked paprika

GLUTEN-FREE OPTION: Substitute 8 ounces of finely chopped tempeh for the seitan.

SOY-FREE OPTION: Substitute coconut aminos and a few pinches of salt for the tamari.

HASH: Heat the oil in a large skillet over medium heat. Stir in the onion and carrot and cook until softened, about 4 minutes. Stir in the potatoes, cover and cook for 4 minutes. Stir in the sprouts, thyme, and salt and cook until sprouts are starting to brown, about 2 minutes.

Stir in 1/4 cup of the broth, cover and cook. Stir in another 1/4 cup of broth, cover and cook until tender, 10 to 15 minutes. Repeat one last time with the remaining broth if the sprouts are not tender. Continue to cook, uncovered, until the bottom of the hash develops a crust, about 2 more minutes, flipping with a sturdy spatula as needed. Season with red pepper flakes, black pepper, and salt to taste.

SEITAN: Heat the oil in a small skillet over medium heat and stir in the seitan. Stir and cook until the seitan is crispy and crunchy, adding 1 teaspoon more oil, if needed, 10 to 15 minutes. The seitan will stick less to the skillet as it dries out and becomes crunchy. Stir in the tamari and paprika and cook until the tamari evaporates, about 1 minute. To serve, divide the hash among the bowls and top with the seitan.

QUICK TIPS: Chop the carrot after you add the onion to the skillet. Chop the potato while the onion and carrot cook. Keep an eye on the seitan to prevent burning.

grits and tomato gravy bowl
with pan-roasted corn

SERVES 3 TO 4 | GF, SFO

Tomato gravy is a staple in Southern cuisine, and it makes for a tasty breakfast bowl. The grits have a lightly smoky flavor and the roasted corn adds another dimension. Using fresh tomatoes in this recipe results in a superior gravy.

1 cup corn kernels, thawed if frozen

GRITS

1 tablespoon olive oil

1/2 medium onion, finely chopped

4 small black cardamom pods

2 garlic cloves, minced

1 cup vegetable broth

1/2 teaspoon sea salt

1 1/4 cups medium-ground corn grits (not instant)

2 cups unsweetened plain nondairy milk, divided

GRAVY

1 tablespoon olive oil

1/2 medium onion, finely chopped

1 teaspoon dried oregano

1/2 teaspoon fresh or dried thyme

1/2 teaspoon salt

Pinch of red pepper flakes

Black pepper

4 medium tomatoes, chopped (4 cups)

2 garlic cloves, minced

2 tablespoons whole-wheat pastry flour or all-purpose flour

2 cups cooked pinto beans

1 cup unsweetened plain nondairy milk

GLUTEN-FREE OPTION: Omit the flour. Mix 1/4 cup of the milk with 1 1/2 tablespoons cornstarch or arrowroot. Add the slurry to the gravy at the end of cooking when the tomatoes are tender; simmer to thicken.

SUBSTITUTION: Substitute 1/2 teaspoon liquid smoke for the black cardamom.

CORN: Heat a large skillet over medium-high heat. Add the corn and cook until golden and roasted, about 7 minutes. Remove from the skillet and set aside.

GRITS: Heat the oil in a medium saucepan over medium-high heat. Add the onion and cardamom. Cover the pan and cook until the onion softens, about 5 minutes, stirring occasionally. Add the garlic, cook for 30 seconds and add the broth and salt. Bring to boil and whisk in the grits.

Continue to whisk until the broth comes back to boil. Whisk in 1 3/4 cups of milk and bring to simmer. Reduce the heat to low and cook until the grits are tender and thick, 10 to 15 minutes. Whisk in the remaining 1/4 cup milk before serving and taste and adjust seasoning. Remove and discard the cardamom.

GRAVY: Heat the oil in the large skillet over medium-high heat. Add the onion, oregano, thyme, salt, red pepper flakes, and black pepper to taste. Cook, stirring occasionally, until the onion is softened, about 4 minutes. Add the tomatoes and garlic. Cook until the tomatoes break down, about 5 more minutes. Stir in the flour and beans. Stir well and add the milk. Bring to boil and reduce to a strong simmer over medium heat. Cook until thickened and the tomatoes are tender, about 10 more minutes. Taste and adjust seasoning.

ASSEMBLY: Serve the grits in bowls with the gravy to the side or over the top. Add the roasted corn.

QUICK TIPS: First, heat the skillet for the corn, then thaw the corn in a strainer under running water and drain well. Chop the onion while the corn cooks. Chop the tomato while the onion cooks.

onion and tomato uttapam bowl
with rice and dal pongal

SERVES 4 | SF

Uttapam is Indian-style pizza, and pongal is a savory breakfast porridge. The uttapam is almost like a pancake and is typically made with fermented dosa batter. Here the process is sped up using yogurt and sourdough bread. The pongal becomes quite thick and is then flavored with spices and cashews. While you could easily serve one or the other, the uttapam can be ready by the time the pongal is. You could also serve the uttapam with any leftover sambar (page 142).

PONGAL

- 3 cups water
- 2/3 cup basmati or other long-grain white rice, rinsed
- 1/2 cup red lentils (masoor dal), picked over and rinsed
- 1/2 teaspoon sea salt

UTTAPAM

- 1/4 cup rolled oats
- 3/4 cups water
- 1/4 cup unsweetened plain vegan yogurt
- 2 cups cubed sourdough bread, crust removed (about 3 slices)
- 1/4 cup chickpea flour
- 1/4 cup whole-wheat pastry flour or all-purpose flour
- 1/2 teaspoon sea salt
- Olive oil, as needed
- 1 small Roma tomatoes, finely chopped
- 1/2 small onion, cut into paper-thin slices
- 1/4 cup minced cilantro

TEMPERING

- 2 tablespoons olive oil
- 2 tablespoons cashew pieces
- 1 teaspoon mustard seeds
- 1 teaspoon cumin seeds
- 1 whole dried red chile or fresh serrano chile
- 1/4 teaspoon asafoetida or 1 teaspoon minced garlic
- 5 to 10 curry leaves (optional)

PONGAL: Combine the water, rice, lentils, and salt in a medium saucepan over high heat. Bring to a boil, reduce to simmer over medium heat and cook until the rice is very tender, about 20 minutes. Using an immersion blender, blend lightly to break up the rice; the pongal will be very thick. Set aside but keep warm.

UTTAPAM: Add the oats to a blender and process into flour. Add the water, yogurt, bread, chickpea flour, pastry flour, and salt. Blend until very smooth. Heat 1 teaspoon of oil in a large skillet over medium-low heat. Add 1/4 cup of batter to the skillet and spread into a 1/4-inch thick circle. Sprinkle on some tomato, onion and cilantro. Repeat with as many pancakes as will fit in the skillet. Drizzle a teaspoon of oil around the pancakes. Cover the pan and cook until golden brown, about 4 minutes. Flip the pancakes and cook an additional minute. Remove the pancakes and set aside. Keep warm.

TEMPERING: Increase the heat to medium and heat the olive oil in the skillet. Add the cashew, mustard and cumin. Stir and cook until the seeds begin to pop and the cashews are golden, about 2 minutes. Add the chile, asafoetida, and curry leaves. Cook for an additional minute and transfer the tempering to the pongal. Stir well, taste and adjust seasoning with salt and black pepper. Serve the pongal with the uttapam.

 QUICK TIPS: First, heat the water for the pongal, then rinse the rice and dal while the water heats. Preheat the skillet while the batter blends.

hungarian breakfast bowl

SERVES 2 TO 3 | GFO, SFO

Hungarians love to eat scrambled eggs with sausage and green bell pepper slices. It is the classic Hungarian breakfast. Here I have replaced the sausage with big cremini mushrooms that are sautéed whole with fennel and red pepper flakes—the same spices used to make sausage.

SCRAMBLE

- 1 tablespoon olive oil
- 1/2 small onion, finely chopped
- 1 medium Anaheim chile, Hungarian wax pepper, or green bell pepper, cut into 1/8-inch rounds
- 1/2 cup grape tomatoes
- 2 garlic cloves, minced
- 1 (14-ounce) package firm or extra-firm tofu, pressed for 10 minutes
- 1/2 teaspoon ground turmeric
- 2 tablespoons vegetable broth
- 1/2 teaspoon Hungarian paprika
- 1/2 teaspoon Indian black salt (optional)
- Sea salt and black pepper
- 4 to 6 slices bread, toasted

MUSHROOMS

- 1 tablespoon olive oil
- 1 teaspoon fennel seeds
- 1/4 teaspoon red pepper flakes
- 2 whole garlic cloves
- 8 ounces cremini mushrooms, stems removed and wiped clean
- 1/2 teaspoon dried sage
- Sea salt and black pepper

GLUTEN-FREE OPTION: Serve with gluten-free bread, toasted.

SOY-FREE OPTION: Substitute 2 cups cooked chickpeas for the tofu. Mash the chickpeas lightly and proceed as for mashed tofu.

SCRAMBLE: Heat the oil in a large skillet over medium heat. Add the onion and cook until golden, about 5 minutes, stirring occasionally. Add the Anaheim chile, tomatoes, and garlic and continue to cook for another 4 minutes, stirring occasionally.

Mash the tofu and add to the vegetables along with the turmeric. Stir and cook until the tofu is golden and dry, about 8 minutes. Stir in the broth and cook until evaporated. Remove from heat, stir in the paprika and optional black salt. Season with sea salt and black pepper.

MUSHROOMS: Heat the oil in a medium skillet over medium heat. Add the fennel, red pepper flakes, and garlic. Add the mushrooms, placing them stem side up. Sprinkle the sage into the mushroom caps. Cook the mushrooms undisturbed until almost tender, 6 to 9 minutes, depending on their size. Flip the mushrooms and continue to cook 5 more minutes. Flip one last time and remove from the heat. Season with the salt and black pepper, to taste. Serve the mushrooms with the scramble and toast.

QUICK TIPS: Begin by pressing the tofu. Chop the onion while the skillets preheat. Remove the stems of the mushrooms while the onion cooks. Chop the pepper and garlic while the onion cooks. Mash the tofu using your hands or a potato masher.

ful medames breakfast bowl

SERVES 3 TO 4 | GFO, SF

Ful medames literally means "stewed fava beans," "ful" meaning "fava beans" in Arabic. This delicious ancient breakfast dish dates back to Egypt's pharaohs. It is slow simmered fava beans with vegetables and olive oil and is served with lemon juice and pita bread. I serve this quick version with a lemon and za'atar-spiced salad and the not-to-be-missed pita bread.

BEANS

- 1 tablespoon olive oil
- 1/2 teaspoon cumin seeds
- 1 small onion, finely chopped
- 1 medium tomato, coarsely chopped
- 1/2 serrano chile, seeded if desired
- 2 garlic cloves, minced
- 2 cups cooked fava beans
- 1/2 cup vegetable broth
- 1/2 teaspoon paprika
- 1/2 teaspoon sea salt
- Black pepper

SALAD

- 1 small tomato, finely chopped
- 1 large radish, cut into 1/8-inch slices
- 1/2 small cucumber, peeled, seeded and finely chopped
- 1/4 small red bell pepper or 2 fresno peppers, finely chopped
- 1/2 serrano chile, minced (optional)
- 2 tablespoons fresh lemon juice
- 1 tablespoon olive oil
- 2 teaspoons za'atar (see Note)
- Sea salt and black pepper
- 2 to 3 pita breads, warmed or toasted

GLUTEN-FREE OPTION: Serve with a gluten-free flatbread instead of the pita.

SUBSTITUTION: Substitute 1 teaspoon toasted sesame seeds, 1/2 teaspoon sumac, 1/2 teaspoon dried thyme, 1/2 teaspoon dried oregano, and 1/2 teaspoon sea salt for the za'atar. Substitute 1/4 teaspoon lemon zest for the sumac, if needed.

BEANS: Heat the oil and cumin in a medium saucepan over medium heat. Add the onion, cover the pan and cook until softened, about 5 minutes, stirring occasionally. Add the tomato, serrano and garlic. Cover and cook until the tomato breaks down, another 3 minutes. Add the beans, broth, paprika, salt and black pepper, to taste. Mash the mixture lightly and cook, stirring occasionally, until the flavors combine and the ful thickens, 8 to 10 minutes.

SALAD: Combine the tomato, radish, cucumber, bell pepper, serrano, if using, lemon juice, olive oil, and za'atar in a medium bowl. Stir well, season to taste with salt, black pepper and za'atar and set aside until needed.

ASSEMBLY: Serve the beans in bowls topped with the salad, including some liquid from the salad and a drizzle of olive oil, if desired. Serve with the pita.

QUICK TIPS: Chop the tomato, serrano, and garlic while the onion cooks. Make the salad while the beans cook.

NOTE: Za'atar is a Middle Eastern spice blend made with dried sumac, sesame seeds, and other ingredients. Za'atar is available online and at international food markets.

congee bowl
with tempeh and scallions

SERVES 4 | GF, SFO

Congee is Asian comfort food at its simplest. It can range from plain to heavily flavored, depending on the cooking broth and the toppings. Lots of delicious and varied stir-ins add a variety of textures and flavors and are the secret to a great congee.

RICE

- 6 cups vegetable broth
- 2/3 cup long-grain white rice, lightly rinsed
- 1 teaspoon natural sugar
- Sea salt and black pepper

TEMPEH

- 2 cups vegetable broth
- 2 teaspoons reduced-sodium tamari
- 1 (2-inch) piece ginger, sliced
- 4 garlic cloves, minced
- 1/4 medium onion, sliced
- 8 ounces tempeh, cut into 1-inch thick slices

GARNISH

- 2 tablespoons grapeseed oil
- 6 garlic cloves, cut into thin slices
- 3 scallions, minced
- Finely sliced fresh ginger

SOY-FREE OPTION: Substitute 3 slices seitan medallions for the tempeh. Cut the seitan into thin slices and sauté in the garlic oil until golden and crisp, about 7 minutes. Season with salt and black pepper. Alternatively, substitute 1 cup of cooked chickpeas, cook until golden and season.

SUBSTITUTION: Replace the tempeh with tofu. Cut 1 (14-ounce) package extra-firm tofu into 1/2-inch slices. No need to simmer the tofu in the broth. Cook the tofu slices in the oil until golden and crisp, about 3 minutes per side. Season with salt and pepper. Cut the fried tofu into 1/4-inch cubes.

RICE: Combine the broth, rice and sugar in a large pot over high heat. Bring to boil and reduce to a strong simmer over medium heat. Cook, stirring occasionally, until the rice is very tender and the broth is reduced by a quarter, about 20 minutes. Using an immersion blender, blend the rice to desired consistency. Taste and adjust seasoning with salt and black pepper. Keep warm and thin with more broth if needed.

TEMPEH: Combine the broth, tamari, ginger, garlic, and onion in a small saucepan over high heat. Bring to boil, reduce to simmer and add the tempeh. Simmer the tempeh for 10 minutes. Set aside until needed.

GARNISH: Heat the oil in a large skillet over medium heat. Add the garlic slices and cook until light golden brown; do not overcook, or the garlic will burn. Drain on paper towels and set aside. Remove the tempeh from the broth and cut into 1/2-inch cubes. Cook the tempeh in the garlic-infused oil until golden brown, about 5 minutes. Drain the tempeh simmering broth and use it to thin the congee, if desired.

ASSEMBLY: Serve the congee garnished with the garlic slices, tempeh, scallions, and ginger.

 QUICK TIPS: First, heat the broth for the rice, then rinse the rice.

ten | build your own bowls

By now you've had a chance to enjoy several of the bowl meals in this book. In fact, you may be thinking about making some of your own bowl creations. To that end, I have provided a handy chart and guidelines on the following pages to help you build great bowls of your own.

Using a few simple suggestions, you'll discover how easy it can be to make your own bowl meals using your favorite ingredients and seasonings.

Following the section on building your own bowls, you will find an ingredient glossary that clearly explains the ingredients used in this book.

how to build your own bowl

It's easy to build your own bowl using your favorite ingredients, just be aware that all combinations don't produce great results. The recipes in *Vegan Bowls* consist of carefully paired flavor combinations, so it's best to begin with these guidelines and chart. The chart (opposite) provides three regional food groups with compatible sub-groups. Begin by choosing a regional type of bowl to build, and familiarize yourself with these suggestions:

1. **STARCH:** Choose 1 starch option. Prepare the starch and set aside.

2. **PROTEIN:** Choose 1 protein option. Prepare the protein as instructed or heat 1 tablespoon grapeseed oil in a large skillet over medium-high heat. (**Note:** your favorite store-bought protein product may be used instead). If using seitan or a store-bought protein, add it to the skillet and cook until golden. Season with salt and black pepper, remove and set aside.

3. **SAUCE:** Choose 1 sauce option. Prepare the sauce according to the recipe instructions. Sauces are normally spooned on top of the finished bowl. However, for Asian bowls, the sauces are stir-fried with the vegetables. (***Note:** for the Sesame Sauce, add 1/4 cup of water to thin it.)

4. **VEGETABLES:** Choose a preparation for the vegetables. Coarsely chop 6 cups of mixed vegetables, cutting denser vegetables smaller than quick-cooking vegetables. For the Asian stir-fries, you also need to make a slurry by combining 2 tablespoons of water and 1 tablespoon cornstarch. Set aside.

    *   **STIR-FRY:** Heat 1 tablespoon grapeseed oil in a large skillet over medium-high heat. Add the vegetables and cook, stirring often, until crisp-tender, about 8 minutes. Add the sauce and cook until the vegetables are tender. Add the slurry and cook until the sauce thickens.
    *   **ROASTING:** Preheat the oven to 450°F. Combine the vegetables, 8 sliced garlic cloves, and 1 tablespoon olive oil on a large baking sheet. Season with salt and black pepper and bake until tender, about 20 minutes, stirring the vegetables midway.
    *   **STEAMING:** Prepare a steamer basket with about 2 inches of water in a large pot over medium-high heat. Add the vegetables and steam until the vegetables are tender, about 10 to 15 minutes. Season with salt and black pepper.

5. **ASSEMBLY:** Divide the starch, protein, and vegetables among 4 bowls. Top with the sauce and garnish as desired.

ASIAN BOWL	EUROPEAN BOWL	LATIN-AMERICAN BOWL
Starch		
30-Minute Brown Rice (p. 16)	4 cups chopped boiled potatoes	30-Minute Brown Rice (p. 16)
3 cups cooked white rice (p. 26)	4 medium baked potatoes	3 cups cooked white rice (p. 26)
8 ounces rice noodles (p. 77)	8 ounces cooked pasta	Couscous (p. 73)
	Perfect Quinoa (p. 16)	Perfect Quinoa (p. 16)
	Polenta (p. 48)	Polenta (p. 48)
	Farro (p. 93)	Farro (p. 93)
Protein		
Fried tofu (p. 74)	Fried tofu (p. 74)	Fried tofu (p. 74)
Lemon Tofu (p. 68)	Marsala Portobello (p. 93)	Southwest Lentils (p. 125)
Garlic-Ginger Tempeh (p. 117)	3 cups cooked beans (any kind)	3 cups cooked pinto or black beans
Edamame, 1 cup, thawed	Chef's Lentils (p. 119)	2 cups chopped seitan
2 cups chopped seitan	Smoky Black Beans (p. 118)	
	2 cups chopped seitan	
Sauce (Use only for stir-frying)		
Sweet and Spicy (p. 26)	Puttanesca (p. 72)	Pumpkin Cream Sauce (p. 55)
Ginger Sauce (p. 29)	Pesto (p. 80)	Pesto (p. 80, use cilantro, not basil)
Sesame Sauce (p. 32)*	Sun-Dried Tomato (p. 93)	Jalapeño BBQ (p. 90)
Indonesian Sauce (p. 65)	Cheese Sauce (p. 58)	Citrus-oregano Dressing (p. 110)
Sambal Grill Sauce (p. 95)	Tahini Sauce (p. 36)	Cheese Sauce (p. 58)
	Lecsó (p. 71)	Chimichurri Sauce (p. 89)
Vegetables (Stir-fry recommended)	(Roasting recommended)	(Steaming recommended)
Bell pepper	Root Vegetables	Kale
Green beans	Broccoli	Broccoli
Mushrooms	Cauliflower	Cauliflower
Bamboo shoots	Summer Squash	Summer Squash
Bok choy	Winter Squash	Winter Squash
Cabbage	Brussels Sprouts	Root Vegetables
Bean Sprouts		
Garnish (as desired)		
Chopped scallions	Mushroom bacon (p. 66)	Roasted corn (p. 160)
Cilantro leaves	Pickled Onions (p. 114)	Cilantro leaves
Basil leaves	Peas, thawed	Chopped avocado
Red pepper flakes	Cashew Sour Cream Sauce (p. 10)	Toasted pepitas
Toasted cashews	Minced parsley	Broken tortilla chips
Toasted sesame seeds	Gremolata (p. 48)	Corn Tortillas (p. 13)
Roasted peanuts		Cashew Sour Cream Sauce (p. 10)

ingredients glossary

oils

Toasted sesame oil: This oil brings a lot of flavor to recipes that include it. It is best to use it judiciously, but in a few recipes the outstanding flavor is welcome.

Grapeseed oil: I use either grapeseed or sunflower oil in all recipes that call for grapeseed oil. Both of these oils have a high smoke-point, which means they can be heated relatively hot before the impurities in the oil begin to burn and, therefore, smoke. Generally, the lighter the oil, the higher the smoke-point; the more refined the oil, the higher the smoke-point. Feel free to use whatever neutral-flavored oil you please.

Olive oil: I use extra-virgin olive oil, but regular olive oil is just as appropriate. Use the best quality you can acquire.

proteins

Tofu: Each recipe indicates which type of tofu is required. None use silken tofu. When pressing the tofu, either use a tofu pressing machine, or wrap the tofu in a lint-free kitchen towel, such as a flour sack towel, and refrigerate overnight. Most of these recipes need a quick press only. Regardless, the tofu press is the best way to do it.

Seitan: Also called "wheat-meat," seitan is made of vital wheat gluten. Store-bought seitan can be costly, so I recommend making your own, for example the Slow-Simmered Seitan, page 11.

Tempeh: This fermented soybean cake has a unique flavor and texture. It is one of the ideal ingredients to substitute with store-bought proteins, if desired.

Beans: Cooking your own beans, preferably using a pressure cooker, is more economical than buying them canned, but it is not always practical. Use 1 (15.5-ounce) can of beans for every 2 cups of cooked beans called for in recipes.

Lentils/dal: Lentils are legumes, and dal is split lentils. Lentils cook quickly. If you cook your own, you can customize them, so I recommend following the recipes rather than using canned lentils. In a pinch, however, canned lentils are better than ordering out. Lentils can be cooked al dente, meaning tender but still holding their shape—or they can be cooked to mush. These recipes require cooking lentils only until they are tender, but still firm and holding their shape. Masoor dal (red split lentils), can cook in about 15 minutes, and it is the only dal I call for in these recipes.

Yogurt: Homemade yogurt is the best! I recognize that homemade is not always possible, but I want to advocate for it. When cooking with store-bought vegan yogurt, please use only soy or coconut, as the flavors of other types still need improvement.

Nondairy milk: Some nondairy milks are very strong and distinct in flavor, such as flax milk. For best results, use soy, almond or rice milk in these recipes. If you are partial to hazelnut or other nut milks, be aware that they bring their own specific flavors to the dishes, sometimes out of place.

Mushrooms: Mushrooms are many and varied. Some are essential to recipes, such as dried porcinis or shiitakes, which have a unique flavor. Portobellos are large and meaty and unique in that sense. Seitan is a great substitute for portobello mushrooms.

Quinoa: Quinoa must be rinsed very well before cooking. Use a very fine mesh or a double fine mesh strainer to wash the quinoa. Rinse it until the water runs clear.

Nuts: Cashews are soft enough to transform into sauces. Most cookbooks soak the nuts overnight, but in these recipes the cashews undergo a quick soak.

Seeds: Sesame seeds and pepitas (pumpkin seeds) add wonderful flavor and texture to dishes. Tahini is ground sesame seeds. Tahini comes in a variety of thicknesses. I use thin-style tahini in these recipes.

Jackfruit: Not really a protein ingredient, as it contains very little protein, it is considered to be a vegan protein replacement, however it is very important to realize that jackfruit that is ripe and yellow-orange is not appropriate for savory applications because it is sweet enough for dessert. Only jackfruit that is young and green and comes stored in brine or water is appropriate for savory dishes. Check the resources for online availability.

grains

Rice (brown, basmati, long-grain, Arborio, paella): While most of these recipes use white long-grain rice, if you have extra time, you may substitute brown rice where a possible substitution is indicated. Arborio rice has a medium grain and paella rice has a short grain. The shorter the grain of rice, the more liquid it absorbs.

Farro: This wheat grain comes in a three varieties, and each variety comes as three different types: pearled, semi-pearled and whole. I use the pearled type in these recipes, as it cooks in around 20 minutes. The best indication of what type of farro you have is the package cooking time. If it's around 20 to 30 minutes, it is most likely pearled farro.

Freekeh: This toasted green wheat contains about twice the protein of other grains. There is whole freekeh and cracked freekeh. These recipes call for the cracked variety. Substitute cracked wheat (bulgur) if you cannot find freekeh; however, the protein content of bulgur is much lower than freekeh's.

Masa harina: This flour is made from lime-soaked corn kernels. It is used mainly to make corn tortillas.

Israeli couscous/regular instant couscous: Couscous is pasta. Israeli couscous is also known as pearl couscous. Regular instant couscous is much smaller than Israeli couscous as it is made with semolina flour and very little water. The grains of semolina are rubbed between the hands to keep them tiny and they are then steamed for hours. The product we purchae in stores is instant couscous because all it needs is to be soaked in a hot, flavored broth.

Polenta and grits: Polenta and grits are a type of ground corn, or cornmeal. The difference between a cornmeal labeled "polenta" or "grits" is the type of corn used. The type of corn determines the flavor and the final texture of the cooked gruel. Polenta cooks up more toothsome and grits or cornmeal cook up creamy. There are also two different kinds of cornmeal labeled "grits," one white and one yellow. White is said to have a milder flavor than yellow. Ultimately, a medium-ground cornmeal or cornmeal labeled "polenta" is ideal in these recipes.

spices and herbs

Black cardamom: This is not to be confused with green cardamom, which has a floral flavor. Black cardamom is smoky and is perfect in savory dishes. Green cardamom is best in sweet dishes. The two are not interchangeable.

Allspice: Make sure your allspice is fresh. If older than six months, the allspice has an off flavor.

Anise: Star anise has a fennel flavor and is vital in the Pho recipe.

Asafoetida: This is an Indian spice that has a mild flavor somewhere between an onion and garlic. If you will be making the Indian recipes in this book, I recommend procuring a small container.

Indian black salt: Also known as kala namak, it is an Indian spice that brings an eggy flavor to tofu and chickpea scrambles.

Sumac: This is a dried fruit that is ground into a purplish powder. It brings a lemony flavor to dishes.

Achiote seeds: Also known as annatto seeds, this seed brings a peppery, tart, light nutmeg flavor to dishes.

Za'atar: A Middle Eastern spice blend consisting of oregano or marjoram, toasted sesame seeds, thyme and sumac, which are tart dried berries. The blend is typically mixed with olive oil and used for dipping warm pita bread. They can be acquired online through Amazon and elsewhere.

flavorings

Chipotle en adobo: Smoked jalapeños packed in a spiced tomato sauce, this condiment adds smoky flavor to dishes along with intense heat. Because the chipotles are packed in a flavored tomato sauce, the peppers also add sweetness to the recipe. You can find them canned in the international aisles of grocery stores.

Coconut milk: Use canned coconut milk, not coconut beverage, which is a completely different ingredient. Coconut milk comes in reduced fat and regular varieties. The reduced fat version contains more water than the regular.

Curry leaves: Used in Indian cooking, these have a unique scent. They give Indian dishes a distinct flavor.

Doenjang: This is Korea's version of miso, a fermented soybean paste. It has a strong flavor, akin to dark or barley miso, which are fermented for about three years.

Galangal or ginger: Galangal is a harsher version of ginger, with a stronger bite.

Gochujang: Korean hot red pepper paste. This pepper paste is made with chiles, glutinous rice, and fermented soybeans. The flavor is pungent, spicy, lightly sweet and complex.

Kaffir lime leaves: These two-lobed leaves bring a light lime flavor to a dish without the acid of citrus.

Lemongrass: This grass has a light and mild lemon flavor without the acid that comes with citrus.

Louisiana-style hot sauce: These hot sauces are made by fermenting cayenne peppers with garlic, vinegar and salt. Frank's Red Hot is the most popular brand available and is responsible for the original buffalo wing sauce. The sauce is spicy but tangy because of the vinegar and fermentation.

Mirin: Japanese sweet rice wine.

Miso: Miso is fermented soybeans and comes in a huge variety of flavors. A type of fungus is used to ferment either soybeans or chickpeas. The fungus is made of either barley or rice and is called koji. The flavors are based on the fermentation length and sweetness of the miso. Light or white miso is sweeter and milder because it is fermented for a shorter period of time. The darker the miso, the saltier it becomes, less sweet, and therefore more robust. Darker misos are fermented for years. I use white or chickpea miso (which is typically soy-free) for most of the recipes in this book.

Paprika: Hungarian paprika is the most well-known and preeminent of the different types of paprika available. Paprika is made of air-dried mild red peppers that are ground and packaged. The fresher your paprika is, the bolder the color will be. Since paprika is made of red peppers, the spice is sweet and true Hungarian paprika is bold in pepper flavor. Hot Hungarian paprika is also available, so care should be taken when purchasing this popular spice.

Preserved lemon: This Moroccan condiment is nothing more than fresh lemons that have been salted and fermented for about a month. It is very easy to make at home, probably easier than to find it in stores. Indian grocers carry a spiced variation of preserved lemons that are referred to as pickled lemons. The Indian version can be highly spiced, depending on the brand.

Red pepper curry paste: A Thai paste of dried red peppers, garlic, ginger, lemongrass, kaffir lime leaves, and onion. This paste is bold and fresh with lemon, lime and pepper flavor. Depending on the type of red peppers used, this paste can be mild or extremely spicy. Take care to check ingredients, as shrimp paste is a common addition. Make your own very easily, page 14.

Sambal oelek: A spicy chili sauce made with vinegar and salt. Unlike sriracha, which is a ready sauce, sambal oelek is more of a cooking sauce. A great alternative is garlic chili sauce, which has the addition of garlic. In spite of the garlic addition, it tastes largely the same as sambal oelek, uncomplicated spice with just a touch of acid.

Seaweed: I only call for one type of seaweed in this book, which is dulse. Dulse is a mild seaweed, perfect for adding some flavors of the sea without overpowering the dish.

Sriracha: This spicy chili sauce made with red chiles, vinegar, sugar and salt is a sweet and spicy table condiment. It is vegan in most cases, but there are a few brands on the market that contain fish sauce. Be sure to check the label.

Sugar: I call for natural sugar in these recipes, which are sugars that are unrefined or minimally refined sweeteners. While I've limited the sugar content in these recipes as much as possible, the need for it in a few recipes is crucial for balancing flavors. When the sweetness from onions, carrots or other whole foods is not enough, I include a small amount of sugar. I use turbinado sugar, which is raw sugar made of crystallized sugar cane juice, but you can use whatever type of sugar you have on hand, including organic vegan cane sugar, Sucanat, organic evaporated cane juice or coconut sugar.

Tamari: The recipes in this book were developed using reduced-sodium tamari. If you use regular tamari or soy sauce, your recipes might be much saltier.

Tamarind: Tamarind is from a pod-like fruit that is tart and sour. It was the inspiration for Worcestershire sauce. Tamarind comes in pulp form, paste form, and concentrate. Concentrate is the most commonly available form, and it is what I use in these recipes. One container lasts for months, even years. If your tamarind is a thick syrup, then it is concentrate.

Vegetable broth: The recipes in this book were developed using an economical store-bought vegetable broth that is mildly flavored, such as store brands like Organic 365 at Whole Foods. I have also included a recipe for Easy Vegetable Broth, page 10. I prepare a batch early in the week and store it in an air-tight container in the refrigerator for use all week long.   The broth also freezes well for up to 6 months.

Vinegars: I use a few varieties of vinegar in this book: rice wine, white wine, white balsamic, apple cider and regular balsamic vinegar. The mildest of the vinegars is rice wine. I have found that vinegar, regardless of its intended mildness, becomes harshly acidic the older it gets. It is important that you taste your vinegar before using it to ensure that it is not harsh and acrid, which could ruin a great dressing or marinade.

acknowledgments

Writing a cookbook is a unique journey unto itself. It is one of trial and error, of late nights, of food that at times doesn't quite hit the mark, of edits and revisions, loads of dishes, bowl meals for breakfast, lunch and dinner, and more than a few teenagers muttering: Bowls again? In spite of all the challenges that a second cookbook brings, it is also an experience that I would repeat without hesitation.

As anyone who has written a cookbook knows, this journey is not a solo one, and many hands make the published work a reality. I am indebted to my home base taste-testers: my children Kati, Mikel and Catt, who were just as supportive this second time around as they were with *Everyday Vegan Eats*.

I am deeply indebted to my incredible husband David who jumped on board with just minor hesitation, knowing full well what was ahead of us for the following year. I am beholden to you, sweetheart!

I am also thankful to the team of spectacular recipe testers who went above and beyond—I am so appreciative of your time, food, and critiques. The testers are the reason why these recipes work universally well in all kitchens, not just my own. I can't thank you enough: Kelly and Mac Cavalier, Dorian Farrow, Liz Wyman, Jenna Patton, Ashlee Wetherington, Claire Desroches, Anna B. Holt and the boys, Jael Baldwin, Ruchama Burrell, Jacqueline Moreno, JJ Sommerville, Desirae Ramsey, Nichole Kraft, and my dear friend Susan Van Cleave. As before, there are no words to properly convey my gratitude.

I am also so very grateful to the team at Vegan Heritage Press who somehow make sense of a bundle of recipes and pages of written text. I am also very grateful to Jon Robertson for taking a chance on me again. If the team at Vegan Heritage Press makes the magic behind the curtain happen, Jon is the wizard behind that curtain, orchestrating it all to work beautifully.

The book you hold in your hands is due to the diligence and talent of all these behind-the-scenes characters. I thank each and every one of you!

about the author

photo by Katelyn Dever

ZSU DEVER has been involved in the restaurant business most of her life. She hails from a long line of culinary professionals and restaurateurs. She is the author of *Everyday Vegan Eats* (published by Vegan Heritage Press) and publishes the blog Zsu's Vegan Pantry. Zsu is a passionate vegan and resides in San Diego, CA, with her three wonderful children, her three adopted adorable felines and her one amazing husband.

Website: www.zsusveganpantry.com
Facebook: https://www.facebook.com/zsuzsanna.dever
Facebook: https://www.facebook.com/ZsusVeganPantry
Facebook: https://www.facebook.com/EverydayVeganEats
Facebook: https://www.facebook.com/VeganBowls
Twitter: https://twitter.com/ZsuDever
Pinterest: http://www.pinterest.com/zsudever/
Instagram: http://instagram.com/zsus_vegan_pantry

Index

Metric Conversions and Equivalents

The recipes in this book have not been tested with metric measurements, so some variations may occur.

LIQUID	
U.S.	METRIC
1 tsp	5 ml
1 tbs	15 ml
2 tbs	30 ml
1/4 cup	60 ml
1/3 cup	75 ml
1/2 cup	120 ml
2/3 cup	150 ml
3/4 cup	180 ml
1 cup	240 ml
1 1/4 cups	300 ml
1 1/3 cups	325 ml
1 1/2 cups	350 ml
1 2/3 cups	375 ml
1 3/4 cups	400 ml
2 cups (1 pint)	475 ml
3 cups	720 ml
4 cups (1 quart)	945 ml

GENERAL METRIC CONVERSION FORMULAS	
Ounces to grams	ounces x 28.35 = grams
Grams to ounces	grams x 0.035 = ounces
Pounds to grams	pounds x 435.5 = grams
Pounds to kilograms	pounds x 0.45 = kilograms
Cups to liters	cups x 0.24 = liters
Fahrenheit to Celsius	(°F - 32) x 5 ÷ 9 = °C
Celsius to Fahrenheit	(°C x 9) ÷ 5 + 32 = °F

WEIGHT	
U.S.	METRIC
1/2 oz	14 g
1 oz	28 g
1 1/2 oz	43 g
2 oz	57 g
21/2 oz	71 g
4 oz	113 g
5 oz	142 g
6 oz	170 g
7 oz	200 g
8 oz (1/2 lb)	227 g
9 oz	255 g
10 oz	284 g
11 oz	312 g
12 oz	340 g
13 oz	368 g
14 oz	400 g
15 oz	425 g
16 oz (1 lb)	454 g

OVEN TEMPERATURE		
°F	Gas Mark	°C
250	1/2	120
275	1	140
300	2	150
325	3	165
350	4	180
375	5	190
400	6	200
425	7	220
450	8	230
475	9	240
500	10	260
550	Broil	290

LENGTH	
U.S.	Metric
1/2 inch	1.25 cm
1 inch	2.5 cm
6 inches	15 cm
8 inches	20 cm
10 inches	25 cm
12 inches	30 cm